To our daughters,
Anna Brown Moore
and
Jordan Brown Byer
You will always be daughters.
Now you are also close friends.

Praise for
Notes from My Father's Bible

Please, take my word for it—you must read Al Brown's book *Notes from My Father's Bible: Taking Some of the Mystery Out of the Mystery*. I could not put this book down. It is truly a page-turner. If you love the Bible or have yearned to know the Bible better, you will love this book. The organization of the different segments invites you to dive right in. The short stories from Al about himself, his family, and his life are a great beginning to one of my favorite reads. The summary explanation of each book of the Bible is instructive and inspiring. The notes from the Bible are unique and convincing. Treat yourself to this book, and you will invest in eternity and find it incredibly enjoyable and enlightening.

—Jim Blanchard, Former Chairman and CEO of Synovus

Notes from My Father's Bible will give you unique insights into reading and understanding the Bible. The text is straightforward and makes even the complicated biblical books interesting and applicable to current everyday living. It will help the beginner as well as the seasoned Bible reader as Al takes each book and explains them in summary form and also gives overall advice in reading God's word. The notes are true gems, and the short stories are amazing and entertaining! This is a treasure for the Brown family, and it will be for you, too.

—John Smoltz, Television Analyst for Turner Sports and the MLB Network, Hall of Fame Baseball Pitcher

I had the great pleasure of meeting Al Brown based on a recommendation from a trusted commercial real estate expert who, like me, has a love for Sea Island and the surrounding area. I simply asked for the best real estate broker, and without hesitation Al Brown was recommended. I was told Al is an even better human being than he is a real estate broker! How true. As I came to know both Al and Gayle, I can say they are remarkable disciples of Jesus Christ. I know that you will be blessed by Al's beautiful stories of God's wonder-working power in his life and his powerful insights into the

Bible. My prayer is that you will have a deeper understanding and love of God's word after reading *Notes from my Father's Bible*.

—Dave Stanchak, Former President of Restoration Hardware, Chief Real Estate and Development Officer

Whether a situation calls for a recommendation on which fishing line to use on a bait-casting reel, specifically in heavy cover, or for asking deep questions about life's many ups and downs, Mr. Al has always been a trusted voice in my life. I appreciate the way he points back to Jesus and the word of God when offering his opinions or advice. His calmness and peacefulness is infectious and has always pulled me closer to the Bible. I hope you enjoy *Notes from My Father's Bible* as much as I have. Everybody needs a Mr. Al in their life. He offers a closeup look at what happens to a life that is centered on the word of God. Enjoy.

—Adam Wainwright, Former St. Louis Cardinals pitcher, Television Analyst for Fox MLB

A Plain Man Looks at the Cross was a popular book during the desperate times of WWII, and the only difference in this reading is the absence of a World War, though some would argue that hostilities, violence, and the casualties of today would compare. Al has shared a plain man's reflections on eternal truths from a genuine love and reverence for the scriptures. His early morning study offers an incomparable collection that his daughters will cherish. His other readers will also gain unforgettable insights. Al Brown has wisely and courageously done his daughters and all of us a great service. Brilliant!

—Dr. Bill Henderson, Black Mountain, North Carolina, Retired Pastor of First Baptist Church, St. Simons Island, Georgia

NOTES FROM MY FATHER'S BIBLE

TAKING SOME OF THE MYSTERY OUT OF THE MYSTERY

AL BROWN

© 2024
Published in the United States by Nurturing Faith, Macon, GA.
Nurturing Faith is a book imprint of Good Faith Media (goodfaithmedia.org).
Library of Congress Cataloging-in-Publication Data is available.

ISBN: 978-1-63528-243-6

All rights reserved. Printed in the United States of America.

Unless otherwise stated, scripture quotes, historical information, and more come from the (NASB®) New American Standard Bible®, Copyright © 1960, 1971, 1977, 1995, 2020 by The Lockman Foundation, used by permission, all rights reserved, lockman.org.

Cover image by Bobby Haven

CONTENTS

Preface: A Letter to My Daughters ix
Introduction xi
    Suggestions for Reading the Bible xi
    Approximate Dates of World Powers in Biblical Times xiii
Part 1: Big Little Things (Short Stories of Life Lessons) 1
    A Preemie Miracle 2
    Two Preemies, One Love Story 3
    A Rose Is a Rose Is a Rose (Or Is It?) 4
    "A Child Shall Lead Them" (Aix-en-Provence, France) 5
    The Worst Seat on the Plane 7
    Praying for and with a Cop in Manhattan 8
    The Ultimate Blink 9
    The Psychic 10
    By Example 13
    Selling a Crime Scene 14
    Losing My Bible 15
    Hearing Directly from God 16
    Never Judge a Book 19
    The Top Five Most Important Days of My Life 20
    Immediate Answered Prayer 21
    Overcoming My Fear of Public Speaking 22
    The Bible Verses that Get Me Through 23
    My Most Memorable Sale 24
    Told Not to Pray 26
    Worn-out Basketball 27
    Perseverance (in Bed) 28
    Discovery of a Talent 29

    Always Trust a Woman's Intuition 31
    The Bible Verse that Changed My Life 33
    A Seven-year-old Teaches Me How to Coach..................................34
    A Weird Way to Cope 35
    Career Decisions 36
    Papa, the Sheep Farmer 37

Part 2: Bible Book Summaries...39
    The Old Testament..40
    The New Testament...53

Part 3: 563 Notes from My Bible 61

Part 4: Favorite Bible Verses 95

Epilogue..99

About the Author...101

Credits/Acknowledgments 102

Special Acknowledgements..103

PREFACE

A Letter to My Daughters

A book's preface typically states its subject, scope, or aims. I have decided to make this preface something of a note to my daughters, Anna and Jordan. The genesis of the book was my desire to instill in them the same kind of love for the Bible that I have enjoyed. The best-selling book in the world should be easy to understand, and I want you, Anna and Jordan, to know and understand the Bible.[1] Out of my desire to do this and to preserve my personal notes, I started transcribing my notes verse by verse, page by page, chapter by chapter. I ended up with a treasure that probably only I could understand.

I regrouped and started a list of notes and truisms that anyone can appreciate. It then occurred to me that my daughters should know some of the experiences your mother and I have had in a life filled with providential opportunities to apply what we believe and practice and to see what God has made of it, molding and directing us along the way.

So here it is, girls, just for you. Remembering our past is essential for directing our future. The Bible uses the word "remember" or its variants more than 500 times. To help you remember, I begin the book with "Big Little Things," a section of stories that show God at work in my life, sometimes in ways too deep to understand at the time they happened. But they all fit together perfectly to form the fabric of who I am and prove once again that God causes all things to work together for good to those who love the Lord (see Romans 8:28).

As I started writing this book, it occurred to me that God, through the Holy Spirit, was directing me to a larger audience who could learn the eternal and practical truths of the Bible. Many people are intimidated by the Bible. I hope you won't mind letting others listen in as I share my heart with you. I want to make the Bible simple to grasp and understand. So in the next section, "Bible Book Summaries," I have tried to summarize each book of the Bible. For some books, I provide key verses that I think reflect the writer's theme.

I wrote this book as a fresh word about the practical use of the Bible that has led one man to an extraordinary love for it. The Bible is practical, personal, poetic, and provocative, and this is a testament of how to read its message without the usual shroud of mystery.

The book is titled *Notes from My Father's Bible*, but the subtitle is *Taking Some of the Mystery Out of the Mystery*. Getting to know the Bible is one of the most important things you will ever do. It will change your life.

I'm a businessman, but my curiosity of the wealth of the Bible has made me a Bible student and learner. The Bible has affected my business life and every other aspect of my life.

I am compelled to tell my story, not because of any success but because of the wonder of God's good leading that has come through the Bible. That is the true success. It is my joy, and it is what I pass on to my family, my friends, and my readers. I hope this book will not only take some of the mystery out of the mystery but also give you hope, direction, energy, wisdom, and peace that we as God's children are meant to have and to help you reach your full potential.

Your dad is far from perfect. A quote from C. S. Lewis is an apt description: "Think of me as a fellow patient in the same hospital who, having been admitted earlier could give some advice."[2] A spiritual world all around you is just waiting to be discovered. A new way of looking at life and your purpose in it can unfold for you. While it is important to know the Bible, it is more important to know its Author.

With this book, I want to help you understand the Bible and its Author. It is a blessing to be your dad.

Al Brown
St. Simons Island, Georgia

NOTES

[1] See "Best-selling book," *Guinness World Records*, https://www.guinnessworldrecords.com/world-records/best-selling-book-of-non-fiction.

[2] C. S. Lewis, "Letter to Sheldon Vanauken," April 22, 1953, in *A Severe Mercy* (London: Hodder & Stoughton, 1977), 134.

INTRODUCTION

This is a book from a father to his two daughters. My original purpose was to preserve my Bible notes and then explain each book of the Bible to them. In addition to my Bible summaries, 563 Bible notes and truisms, and my favorite verses (Parts 2–4), I include short stories of my life and some of the unique and providential life lessons my wife Gayle and I have experienced in our fifty-two years together (Part 1). We moved to St. Simons Island, Georgia, in 1972 after getting married. We emptied our bank account, all $301 of it, rented the smallest U-Haul possible, and left our hometown of Elberton, Georgia, to start our lives together. In these pages you will read about experiences as varied as encountering a psychic to selling a crime scene to losing a child and my religion. Some experiences were miraculous, some whimsical, and all true and impactful. Get ready to read some new things about God and the Bible, and prepare to be uplifted and blessed.

SUGGESTIONS FOR READING THE BIBLE

After reading through the entire Bible for the first time, I analyzed ways to make it easier for me to understand and to clarify the message intended by a particular passage or book. This worked well for me. I hope these suggestions will do the same for you.

1. Before starting, always say a prayer asking the Holy Spirit for teaching, explanation, and guidance.

2. To better understand God, read the Bible for a better grasp of the spirit world and of God's holiness.

3. In reading and understanding the Bible, filter every Scripture through Jesus, asking yourself what He said about each idea or situation. He is the starting place and the ending place for everything.

4. I suggest that beginning Bible readers start with one or more of the following:
- Mark
- Matthew 5–7
- Philippians
- 1 John
- Luke
- Acts
- John

5. Genesis 1–11 sets the stage for the biblical story and helps us understand the entire Bible, both Old and New Testaments. God is revealed as Creator, our loving Father/Parent, the Provider, and a just Judge. Satan introduces sin into God's perfect creation. God, being holy, cannot and will not tolerate sin.

6. The central event in the Old Testament is the exodus, when God used Moses to lead the enslaved Hebrew people out of Egypt (see Exodus 1–14).

7. Without Leviticus, the powerful message of the cross is not fully understood because the book teaches about God's law of burnt offerings and sacrifices of atonement.

8. The most important chapter in the Bible is possibly John 20, where Jesus's empty tomb is discovered. He is alive!

9. In the simplest terms, the Old Testament is about the nation of Israel, and the New Testament is about a man named Jesus. The nation had to be formed to bring forth the Man.

10. Don't focus so much on a few words or verses that you miss the message of the whole text. Don't get hung up on the small stuff.

11. Look at each Scripture in the context of the situation, the writer, and the purpose of that particular book. This book will offer guidance to assist you.

12. Complete understanding of Scripture is not necessary.

13. Remember that some of people's ideas in the Bible are not God's ideas (for example, the ideas in Ecclesiastes were written by a man looking back on his life, much of which he lived apart from God).

14. There are different uses of language in the Bible: symbolic, idiomatic (non-literal), exaggeration, sarcasm, humor, metaphors, and similes. It's not all literal.

15. The Bible contains cultural truths as well as spiritual and eternal truths.

16. Terms and expressions in the Bible can have different meanings from everyday usage. Even certain English words have changed meaning in our lifetime. Use your God-given common sense.

17. Jesus used logic and not emotion in his attempts to teach and persuade.

18. Jesus doesn't answer the "why" questions.

19. God is not limited by time or space.

20. Much of the Bible contrasts those who live for God with those who don't.

21. You will never know God except the God you know yourself.

APPROXIMATE DATES OF WORLD POWERS IN BIBLICAL TIMES

I refer to different periods of time in this book. Here is a convenient list of world powers in biblical times.

- Egyptian Empire: 2000–1200 BC

- Assyrian Empire: 1076–612 BC

- The Assyrians destroyed the northern kingdom of Israel in 721–722 BC.

- Babylonian Empire: 612–539 BC

- Judah fell in 597 BC, and the Babylonians destroyed Jerusalem in 586 BC.

- Persian Empire: 539–332 BC

- The Persians permitted the Jews to return to their homeland from exile in Babylon.

- Greek Empire: 332–146

- The foundation was laid for the Greek translation of the Bible.

- Roman Empire: 146 BC–AD 476

- Christ appeared, and the church was formed. The Roman Empire legalized Christian worship in AD 313. In AD 526, Emperor Justinian made Christianity a universal religion over what had been the Roman world when he had the calendar changed to reckon time from the birth of Christ rather than the founding of Rome.

PART 1

Big Little Things
(Short Stories of Life Lessons)

Part 1 includes a number of personal short stories about my life experiences and how I applied the Bible's truths and direction as I went through them. Jesus was a master at teaching through short stories and parables, and the messages are memorable and instructive. Hopefully, my stories will be the same for you.

A Preemie Miracle

After coming into the world two and a half months early, weighing two pounds and fifteen ounces, our daughter Anna Brown dropped in weight to two pounds, ten and a half ounces as she fought for her life. The neonatal nurses and doctors told us later how sick she really was and how they feared she would not survive. Being professionals, they never showed this fear on their faces or in their attitudes.

Gayle and I spent every weekend in Savannah, Georgia, and drove the one hour, thirty-minute trip from St. Simons Island two additional times during the week. But on one occasion, after nearly two and a half months in the hospital, Anna took a turn for the worse. After the medical professionals did everything they could for our baby girl, we left the hospital late that night to return home, thinking we would have to endure another funeral with a very small casket.

As we headed south on I-95, I snapped. Reflecting on the earlier death of our first daughter at three days old and our dashed hopes to start a family, I had all I could take. Thinking we were about to lose Anna after all we had been through, I cursed God out loud and even proclaimed to Gayle that now we know the truth about God: God doesn't even exist. I felt a strange sense of relief that I had finally come to the truth because no loving God would allow this needless suffering. I went to sleep that night thinking I would live the rest of my life "unshackled" by religious beliefs. That was my plan.

God had another one.

Early the next morning, we received a call from an excited nurse: "You won't believe how Anna is today! She's doing great, breathing some room air, and has very good color!" We made record time getting to the hospital to witness the day that Anna turned the corner toward her discharge when we could finally, mercifully, take her home.

My talk with God that day was humbling and embarrassing for me. God showed me that despite my weak faith, He didn't leave me. God didn't need me or my prayers to perform a miracle, and that drew me closer to Him than I had ever been. I fully realized that I could do nothing to make God love me any more or any less. From that point on, at age twenty-seven, I truly began to build my faith on the Rock and not on the shifting sands where it had been (see Matthew 7:24-27). It was now real.

Two Preemies, One Love Story

On June 23, 1924, Herman and Grace Brown were desperate. Their baby was in a hurry to come into the world some two and a half months early. They hurried to Emory Hospital in Atlanta, about 100 miles from the farm in Elberton, Georgia. In that day and time, neonatal units were nonexistent, and my grandparents headed for the best hospital they knew. Allen Brown, my daddy, was born that night, weighing right at three pounds. His mother died giving birth to him. So here was Herman, a sheep farmer and cotton buyer, with a helpless and sick baby boy.

The folks at Emory did all they could and provided a nurse to accompany Papa and his tiny baby, carried in a shoebox, on the train ride back to Elberton. Papa was told they were sending the baby home to die. But God had other plans. My daddy survived and thrived. Papa fell in love with the nurse, and she became my Mema, the grandmother I loved and adored, creating one of the greatest love stories. I get chills and tears every time I think about it.

I suppose there is another part to this story. In 1978, Gayle and I were in an ambulance headed to the neonatal center of Memorial Medical Hospital in Savannah, Georgia, with a baby on the way at thirty-one weeks. On my daddy's birthday, June 23, our daughter Anna Brown came into the world two and a half months too soon, tipping the scales at two pounds, fifteen ounces. It took Anna more than two months to get to four and a half pounds, when Memorial Medical's terrific neonatal unit let us take her home to St. Simons Island, Georgia. Today, she is a happy, healthy mother of Parker Felton Moore, our seven-year-old grandson.

A Rose Is a Rose Is a Rose (Or Is It?)

When Gayle and I travel, we always take our Bibles. In 2008, we took a trip to London, Paris, and Aix-en-Provence, France. In Cap d'Antibes, a coastal village in France, we stayed at a little inn called Villa Val des Roses. After checking in and unpacking, we set our Bibles in the room and thought nothing of that simple act until the second morning of our stay (October 12). Returning from breakfast, we found a handwritten note from the housekeeper. She had a simple request: "Please help me to pray about my life." She wrote that she was reminded that it was Sunday when she saw our Bibles. She was unable to go to church on Sundays due to her work. She signed it, "Thanks. And God Bless. Rose."

We did not see her until the following morning at breakfast. We smiled, spoke, and invited her to our room for prayer. I don't remember specifically what I prayed, but the Holy Spirit did all the heavy lifting. When I heard Rose and Gayle sobbing, I knew the needed spiritual care was being provided. I'm certainly not qualified for such a task; I was all we had, and the Lord used me. All three of us embraced as Gayle and I promised to pray for Rose daily, and we have done so faithfully for fifteen years. She is still on my prayer list.

As we said our goodbyes, Gayle happened to glance down, and her eyes fell upon a book she had brought to read and study: *The Power of a Praying Woman* by Stormie Omartian.[1] She gave the book to Rose.

As beloved radio host Paul Harvey would say, "And now for the rest of the story." On April 4, 2011, Gayle received an email: "Hi Madame, thanks for your book that you gave to me! I don't know if you remember me, I'm Rose, working in the hotel in Cap d'Antibes! Thank you. With your prayers, I'm happy because I am using your book for teaching groups, and I am now in a church in Cannes, France!"

Neither Gayle nor I could contain our joy. Learning that Rose, who had needed help to pray, was now teaching others to pray was a big "wow moment" for us. We found it so humbling that God could use us in this way on the other side of the world.

Never underestimate your actions and what God can do with them.

---

[1] Stormie Omartian, *The Power of a Praying Woman* (1997; repr., Harvest House Publishers, 2014).

"A Little Child Shall Lead Them" (Aix-en-Provence, France)

On the last night of our stay in France, we were running low on money, so we took to the streets to find an inexpensive place for dinner. As we almost stopped at a restaurant, something told us to look at one more spot. The prices were reasonable, the menu looked good, and there was an available table for two, so we took it.

As we talked and ordered wine for the meal, the nice lady next to us heard our accents and asked where we were from. I told her we lived in St. Simons Island, Georgia, and she immediately responded, "Do you know where Eulonia is?" I made her repeat the question, incredulous that she knew of this teeny-tiny place in such a rural, remote area of Georgia. It turns out that this lady had attended a Gullah Geechee ring shout there.[1] At that point, I started asking her questions. How did this come about? Who are you? What's your story?!

Dr. Diane Komp was a pediatric oncologist. Educated at Yale University, she had joined the Yale faculty in 1978 and at the time of our encounter was a professor in pediatric hematology and oncology at the University of Virginia. She discovered Eulonia after becoming interested in the culture and language of the Gullah, an African American ethnic group living predominantly in the low country regions of Georgia, South Carolina, North Carolina, and Florida.

When she told us about a mission trip she had taken to Sierra Leone, I stopped her abruptly to ask how a busy doctor in her position could go on a mission trip. It didn't fit the profession and her educational background. She shared with Gayle and me her conversion experience to Christianity. Her path began in disbelief. When she started in pediatrics, she vacillated between being an agnostic and an atheist (as described in her book *Children Are…Images of Grace*).[2] Her clinical mentor advised her not to get close to her patients, many of whom would die. The reason to do your work and concentrate on being a good doctor, not to deal with feelings. His advice at the time seemed good to her, so she tried to keep her feelings as "numb" as possible. As a side effect of this approach, her faith slipped further and further away with each child who passed.

Then strange things began to happen. Children with serious, life-taking illnesses do not often pass from this life without some warning sign. Many times, nursing staff or parents alerted Dr. Komp so she could be bedside for that moment. Time after time, she told us of dying children who would say that they saw angels, proclaim their beauty, and delight in their beautiful singing. On some occasions children saw visions of Jesus and then lay back on the pillow and died. Some of the children were just a few years old and not from a Christian upbringing or home.

"Dr. Di" found this testimony the most reliable witness. The children converted her. She saw God's love through Jesus and angels bringing peace and comfort. The spiritual experiences surrounding the deaths of these children were real and pure and innocent. As the prophet Isaiah wrote, "a little child shall lead them" (Isaiah 11:6).

Gayle and I will never forget Dr. Diane Komp, her story, and the experiences of some of her patients. At one time or another, we all need help with our faith. Dr. Di has provided a reservoir from which we have drawn deeply over the years since our providential meeting in France. She gave us a precious gift that evening.

---

[1] The Gullah Geechee people were African descendants whose ancestors brought to America a rich heritage of African cultural traditions in art, music, crafts, and food. The ring shout was one of these traditions. Learn more at "The Gullah Geechee," *Gullah Geechee Cultural Heritage Corridor Commission*, https://gullahgeecheecorridor.org/thegullahgeechee/.

[2] Diane Komp, *Children Are…Images of Grace: A Pediatrician's Trilogy of Faith, Hope, and Love* (Zondervan, 1996).

The Worst Seat on the Plane

In May 2005, my associate Nick Doster and I boarded a Delta jet in Atlanta bound for New Orleans. Nick and I worked for Sea Island Company, and we were giving a luncheon presentation to a group at Galatoire's. (Just thinking about it now makes my mouth water!) As we searched for our seats, Nick (the Trick) got a good window seat close to the front. As I trudged on, it became obvious that mine was all the way back: the middle seat with the bathroom directly behind me. Bummer. But I soon discovered God picked out that seat for me.

Since I teach an adult Sunday school class every week, I got out my book and Bible to study the upcoming lesson, minding my own business. Before the plane started down the runway, a flight attendant took the aisle seat beside me. After we leveled off and before cabin service started, she noticed what I was doing and asked me to write the Scripture down for her. After the carts were cleared from the aisle, she came right back to her seat, interested in the lesson and the Scripture.

It turned out that she had a spiritual thirst and needed prayer, and once again, I was all she had at that moment. God used me to be His hands and feet. What started as the worst seat on the plane turned out to be the best seat I ever had. I still pray for that woman daily, though I'll probably never see her again this side of Heaven.

Praying for and with a Cop in Manhattan

My wife Gayle likes to shop. I knew I was in trouble on our honeymoon in 1972 when I discovered she had memorized her credit card number. She still does that today.

We used to love traveling to New York, the "greatest city in the world," as my New York friends call it. We loved the shows, the restaurants, the people, the energy, and the sights. Gayle loved the shopping. Some years ago in NYC, we ate breakfast and then walked and walked, looking for Saks Fifth Avenue. We came upon a policeman, a gentleman of color, and asked him for directions. With a mischievous look, he replied, "Oh, you do not want to know how to go there!" I looked him square in the eyes and proclaimed, "I like you!" Upon striking up a conversation with him, I learned he was studying to become a deacon in his church. I immediately asked if I could pray for him. Somewhat taken aback, he said yes. So Gayle and I put our arms around him, and right in front of God, Manhattan, and everybody, I laid a Spirit-led prayer on this cop and his family that surprised even me. He sincerely thanked us, obviously touched. Walking away, I laughed out loud and said to Gayle, "Can you imagine what he will tell his wife tonight? 'Honey, you won't believe what these two white folks from the South did for me today!'"

The Ultimate Blink

Malcolm Gladwell wrote a book titled *Blink*.[1] It's about how people make decisions. He thinks, and I agree with him, that people make decisions in the span of a blink, about two seconds, whether we realize it or not. Let me give you a real-life example.

In summer 1967, in a small gym in Elberton, Georgia, I shyly asked a girl to dance. It was most enjoyable, and it ended way too soon. I thanked her and went back to sit with my friends, thinking no more about it. She walked straight over to her best friend and told her she had just danced with the boy she was going to marry. She was right. Five years later, Gayle Cleveland became Gayle Brown. She had a better "blink" than I did. Fifty-two years later, we are still dancing.

I've learned to trust women's intuition ever since, especially Gayle's. We lost our first baby girl after three days. Then, with our daughter Anna, Gayle's pregnancy was complicated and baffled the doctors. Gayle told her doctors what the problem was: she had an incompetent cervix that needed stitching. They scoffed at the idea, she insisted, and it turned out she was right again. That's why we have our daughters Anna and Jordan, who are in their forties as I write this.

Test yourself and be honest. Some of us don't make good blink decisions. Often, our "blink" on the Bible is that it's a hard book to read and understand and that it's irrelevant and not important or necessary. A second look, deeper and probing, reveals otherwise.

One other thing: always trust a woman's intuition!

[1] Malcolm Gladwell, *Blink: The Power of Thinking without Thinking* (Back Bay Books, 2005).

The Psychic

I went to see a psychic.

I have never experimented with drugs, but if I had, I would tell you about it and tell you *not* to do it! But I did do something that I shouldn't have done, so I'll preface the story with this admonition: "Don't do what I did."

In 1981, I went to see one of Atlanta's "leading psychics." I read about her in a magazine article by a skeptical journalist who described in detail his experiences with three different psychics. One lady impressed him most with her insight and 80 percent accuracy. I was curious and intrigued but should have heeded the ominous visit he got afterwards from an evil spirit.

In addition to being curious about whether psychics were truly gifted with foresight, I faced a few important business decisions and needed help to make them. The main choice was whether to leave a managing broker position to join Sea Island Company in their real estate department. I thought I heard God's direction to make the move, but I wanted more assurance.

After scheduling the appointment, I drove five hours to Atlanta. Already apprehensive and nervous, I was surprised to find a waiting room full of people. When my time came and my name was called, I took a seat in the psychic's comfortable office. We offered the perfunctory greetings, and she asked the purpose of my visit. I sheepishly told her the truth. I was there to check out her profession and her ability. She laughed and started asking me a few questions: When is your birthday? Where is your place of birth? Where did you grow up? Where do you live now? She asked the same questions about Gayle, our children, our parents, and our grandparents. I gave her the information as well as I knew it. I didn't know some of the information about grandparents, though I thought to myself, "Aren't *you* supposed to know these things?"

She closed her eyes and proceeded to share information about me that no one could know, some general and some specific. I was dumbfounded. Then, she moved on to Gayle and to other family members I had asked about. At that point, she had my attention and complete focus.

She started to tell me about my future and the future of some of the family. I'll give you two examples, one a big miss and the other amazingly accurate.

The "miss" involved our family. The psychic said she "saw" that Gayle had lots of trouble with her pregnancy. She couldn't determine what it was, so I told her about losing our first baby at three days old and Anna coming two and a half months early as a very sick preemie. The psychic advised us not to have any more children, saying that Gayle's life and health would be in danger. "Too late", I told her. We were expecting. She cringed, took a deep breath, and waited a moment. The she finally spoke. "Gayle will be okay, and this will be a successful delivery." Of course, I had to ask: "Boy or girl?" She said she was not good at that, but she saw a dark-haired boy. Then, she chuckled and said this child would be a handful for Gayle. (That part was accurate!)

The prediction she got right related to a question from me. I asked about my daddy, who was fifty-seven years old at the time. How long would he live? What would cause his death? Without hesitation, she said he would die at sixty-four years of age from heart problems. Unfortunately, she got that one exactly right.

I saw this psychic one more time when she visited St. Simons Island. Shortly after that appointment, I discovered the danger of dealing with matters of the occult. One day I was at home by myself in our family room. The room suddenly got freezing cold, and I felt a strong, unmistakable evil presence. I literally ran out of the house and into the backyard, visibly shaken. I composed myself enough to say out loud: "In the name of Jesus, leave me alone! Get away from me!" In that instant, the evil spirit left me.

I never went back to the psychic, and I never had another evil spirit approach me that way.

It was a frightening experience that scared me to my senses. What did I learn?

I learned that the Bible warns against dabbling in the mystical occult arts, and we should take these warnings seriously (see Ephesians 6:11-12 and Deuteronomy 18:9-12a). These practices are of Satan. The devil is real. Occult practices lead us away from God. For the people in that psychic's waiting room, she was "their god."

Satan submits to the name of Jesus, the name above every name. The Gospel of Matthew gives an account of Jesus being tempted at Matthew 4:10. Satan submits to Jesus's command to leave. In Mark 9:25-26, an evil spirt obeys Jesus. If you are approached by an evil spirit, command him to leave you in the name of Jesus. It works 100 percent of the time. Satan and his demonic forces flee from the name of Jesus Christ. (Dr. Scott Peck in his book *People of the Lie*[1] highlights this fact from his personal experience.)

There are some things we are just not supposed to know. Instead, we are to trust God with everything, especially the future.

James 4:8 states, "Draw near to God, and he will draw near to you." The same principle applies if we draw near to the evil one.

Don't make the same mistake I did.

[1] M. Scott Peck, *People of the Lie: The Hope for Healing Human Evil* (Simon & Schuster, 1983).

By Example

Maurice Freeman and I are brothers. He is a huge black man, and I am a pretty average white guy, but we are brothers from different mothers. We call each other brother. Maurice is a high school football head coach at Quitman in Brooks County, Georgia. He's one of the top coaches in Georgia and has more than 200 wins to prove it. His coaching lessons go far beyond football. Coach Freeman is a true mentor. He cares for and molds young men, many from poverty-stricken and challenged backgrounds, who live in a county burdened with a high poverty rate and fractured families.

Two years ago on a Thursday, I got a call from Maurice: "Hey, brother! What are you doing tomorrow evening? I'm bringing my football team to Epworth on St. Simons, and I need a motivational speaker tomorrow." I immediately said yes, wondering what I would say and why I agreed so quickly.

My talk went fine, I think. As I looked into the eyes and hearts of these young men, I wanted success for their lives. They have so much promise, but the odds seem stacked against them. Maurice walked with me to my car, and I asked him what he and "his guys" would do for the remainder of the weekend. On Saturday, they would go to the beach and see something they had never seen: the ocean. Then, they would eat seafood. He said he had something special planned for Saturday night: they would go back to the meeting room and Maurice would do a crazy, outrageous, magnificent thing: he would wash their feet.

That act, following the example of Jesus (see John 13), must have had a huge impact on the rough-and-tough football players. No wonder the players revere Maurice Freeman.

And by the way, they won the state championship that year. Isn't God good?

Selling a Crime Scene

As I showed the house, it was obvious the couple loved it. This was early in my second career after starting my own real estate company, and I needed the sale in the price range of $1,500,000. After we finished the showing, they said they wanted to buy the home. As we paused in the great room before I turned off the lights, I asked a question: "Would it bother you to live in a house where a murder was committed?" The wife, an attorney, laughed and said, "Of course not!" I looked at the husband and saw that the blood had drained from his face. He stammered, "I don't know." I explained to them that over thirty years ago, a murder had occurred in this house. In fact, it was a double murder of the couple who lived there. I advised them to think about it overnight. The next day, they called and said they couldn't buy a murder house and thanked me for telling them. They returned to their Tennessee home, and I figured I'd never hear from them again.

Several years later, my wife Gayle and I were having a quiet Friday dinner together when the phone rang. I don't always take calls at dinner, but I answered this one. The man identified himself and told me about a house he wanted to buy. I had no idea who he was but agreed to help him and his wife. We negotiated a price over the phone and met later as they came to finalize details. I asked them why they chose me as the Realtor to represent them. They shared a conversation that went something like this:

Husband: "Who should we call to help us?"

Wife: "Why don't we call that guy—I can't remember his name—who told us about the murder house?"

That series of events led to more than one sale, but more importantly, it led to my becoming great friends with two of the finest people I have met in my fifty-two years in the real estate business.

Here's the moral of the story: always be honest, and tell all the important things you think someone might want to know, even if it is not required. It pays off in more ways than you can imagine.

Losing My Bible

My personal Bible is *The Open Bible* edition of the New American Standard Bible.[1] The words of Christ appear in red font. The edition includes translations, study notes, a cyclopedic index, and a concordance. Gayle, Anna, and Jordan gave me this Bible as a birthday gift on September 29, 1984. I have come to love it. By far, it is the most treasured possession I own (yes, Gayle, even more treasured than my bass boat!).

A handsome, durable leather cover now protects my Bible, but if you looked through it, you would see torn pages and smeared ink.

One Thursday morning, I woke up and got a cup of coffee to start my early morning ritual of Bible reading. But I couldn't find my Bible. I looked everywhere and panicked a little. By lunchtime, still no sign of it. I called our pastor, Dr. Bill Henderson, and told him I had a prayer request he had never heard before. I had lost my most treasured, sacred book, and I wanted his prayers. He wholeheartedly agreed, probably somewhat relieved at the request.

I began to have clarity about where it might be. The evening before, we had gone to Wednesday night church supper. I remembered placing my Bible on the trunk lid of the car while I put something in the back seat. I thought about where the car had traveled since then. I had driven to Brunswick, the port city of our county, on the causeway that crosses four-plus miles of salt marsh and five bridges, including one over the intracoastal waterway! To make matters worse, it had rained the night before.

Bill and I prayed, and then I took off looking. As I got near the top of the tallest bridge, I saw something flapping in the wind, open to the heavens above as if proclaiming the gospel to the world. My precious Bible! I couldn't believe it. I slammed on the brakes, jumped out of the car, and scooped it up—torn, somewhat tattered, and wet but intact. Some of the ink notes were smeared, giving the appearance of blood stains in some places. Appropriate, I thought.

I clutched the Bible to my chest like it was a million-dollar bill. The next day, the leather cover was on order, and I haven't lost my Bible again.

[1] *The Open Bible*, NASB (Thomas Nelson, 1979).

Hearing Directly from God

Let's get something straight. I am not a religious kook. I'm a pretty normal guy. Those who know me know that I start each day with coffee and a prayer and Bible reading, and I end each day with a glass of bourbon.

If you were to tell me the story I'm about to tell you, I'm not sure I would believe you. With one word, God spoke directly and audibly to me as clearly as a person standing right next to me.

By 2012, I had worked for Sea Island Company for more than thirty years. I was Senior Vice President of Real Estate and had a solid six-figure income with full benefits, health insurance, and club memberships paid for by the company. I was sixty-two years old with little debt, stable income, and a bright future. My family and I were "comfortable," which suited me because I always considered myself risk averse. But in 2011 and 2012, a few things happened that made me unsettled about "coasting and paddling in" as I approached a normal retirement age.

People say if you want to hear God laugh, tell him your plans. Some years ago, I told God my plans: retire at sixty-two to play and fish for the rest of my life, drawing generous monthly checks from Social Security and a pension, after cashing in my stock rights, of several million dollars accrued from years at Sea Island Company. That started to change and unravel in 2008. The financial world went south that year, and the company fortunes went with it. Sea Island, the company everyone thought was invincible since its start in 1926, was going broke. With tons of debt, back notes due, and a dwindling income stream from real estate and resort revenue, the writing was on the wall. The rumors started in 2009, and by December 2010, Sea Island Company was sold out of bankruptcy.

It was a sad day when I had to go home and tell Gayle that our retirement nest egg was worthless, and my pension would be cut in half after being taken over by Benefit Guarantee Corporation. Financially, we essentially had to start over. My net worth declined by 84 percent. Romans 8:28 seemed like a distant dream: "And we know that God causes all things to work together for good to those who love God, to those who are called according to His purpose" (NASB). But you know what? That's exactly what happened. These events lead to my decision to form my own real estate company in 2013, and it happened like this.

From 2011 through 2012, I started hearing a still, small voice, sort of a whisper. It was really a thought in my mind at that stage. I willed it to go away. It was a crazy idea and would involve borrowing several hundred thousand dollars at a high interest rate. Venture capital doesn't come cheaply. This would put everything I owned at risk, something I promised myself I would never do. But the thought wouldn't go away. It got to the point where I sensed a calling to do this. Every day, I went out by the lake we live on and knelt in prayer, ending the prayer each time in the form of Proverbs 3:5-6: "Trust in the LORD with all your heart, and do not lean on your own understanding. In all your ways, acknowledge Him, and He will make your paths straight" (NASB). One evening in early spring 2012, as I repeated the verse and started to rise from my knees, I heard, audibly and clearly, a command: "Go!" That frightened me back to my knees. Trembling, I got up again and went directly to Gayle in the house. "Honey, we're going. I'm leaving and going out on my own, and here's why: God told me to!" Gayle didn't hesitate and stated firmly and bravely, "Well, that settles that."

I slept well that night but woke up wanting a little more assurance. Where could I possibly get it? A thought came to me. Go see Wayne Huizenga, the most successful entrepreneur in the history of American business. He is the only person to start and take three businesses to Fortune 500 companies: Waste Management, Blockbuster, and AutoNation. Plus, he had ownership of various sports teams in Miami including the Dolphins (National Football League), Marlins (National League Baseball), and Panthers (National Hockey League). Surely, he would applaud my willingness to start a company and grow it. I called Wayne and went to his home. We sat down, and I proudly told him what I planned to do and asked his opinion and advice. Imagine my shock and dismay when he looked me dead in the eyes and said, "Don't do it." His reasoning was about the established great companies already in the business, the challenging environment of the business, and the economic outlook in 2012 and the foreseeable future. I stared back into the eyes of this great man and said, "Wayne, I've got to do it." He asked me why, and I said, "God told me to." Wayne replied, "Well, then you do have to, Al."

That settled it once and for all. I found a shell of an office space, contracted to build it out, and signed a five-year lease. I worked on a budget for my first year (salaries, office equipment, supplies, advertising, real estate and MLS dues, loan interest, insurance, telephones, etc.), and my head spun when I totaled it up. It came to a little over $40,000…monthly. Every day the sun came up, I would owe about $1,350. I put the budget in a file and wrote on the cover, "Don't look down." For the first five months, I was awakened at 3:00 a.m. by what I called the "night demons." They reminded me of my terrible mistake. Then I got up between 4:30 and 5:00 a.m. to start my day. Around 7:00 or 7:30 each night, Gayle called to tell me dinner was about ready and to come home. Each Saturday morning by the time the sun came up, I had cleaned the office and was headed home to shower so I could get back to the office.

Fast-forward to today, eleven years after starting my company. I have been blessed beyond my wildest dreams. My little company has a significant market share, greatly exceeding much larger companies, and last year, I sold the highest-priced residential home in the history of the state of Georgia. All for God's glory.

As it turns out, God had a bigger plan for my life than money and success. He showed me that the reason for this blessing was to give it away. That led to the establishment of the ABCo Initiative, a philanthropic division of Al Brown Company, headed up by our daughter Jordan, who has the gift of helping others. With a focus on special needs children and adults, and other individuals and organizations, we are helping meet needs (physical, emotional, spiritual, and monetary) that many don't even know exist.

The Bible on my credenza is opened to Proverbs 16:3: "Commit your works to the LORD, and your plans will be established." Soli Deo Gloria (Glory to God alone).

Never Judge a Book

Back in the 1980s when I worked for Sea Island Company as a real estate broker, our receptionist was a great lady named Alice Ramsburg. Alice was married to a Lutheran minister. She related well to our clientele. With her nice, outgoing personality, she greeted the public warmly and comfortably. She always showed up on time and wasn't in a rush to go at 5:00 p.m. Despite being from the Northeast, Alice fit in well, exhibiting our southern hospitality with one glaring exception: she referred to soft drinks as "pop." The first time I heard her say this, I called her aside to explain that Southerners offer folks not "pop" but a "Coca-Cola" or "Co-Cola." She tried but couldn't say "Co-Cola." It just wouldn't come out of her mouth. But I did finally break her of saying "pop."

Anyway, that's not the story. One day, Alice called me from her lobby desk in a panic. She said there was a real "character" standing around outside: rough-looking, smoking a cigarette, with disheveled hair, unshaven, wearing a t-shirt and wrinkled clothes. She said she was thinking of locking the door and calling security. I told her to let him in. "He's Willis Everette," I told her. Willis was the founder of Invesco and one of the wealthiest clients we ever had. (He bought an oceanfront home the next day).

The Top Five Most Important Days of My Life

In summer 2012, Sea Island Company had an offsite meeting on Kiawah Island for its officers. We took part in a thought-provoking exercise. Our facilitator asked us all to write down the five most important days of our entire lives. Here is what I wrote:

#4 and #5—When our daughters were born.

#3—Marrying Gayle.

#2—The day I read John 14:23 and it turned my spiritual life around, putting me on a path to seeking spiritual truths and developing a deeper relation with God, my Creator and Savior.

#1—Today. This day is all I have. Yesterday is gone; tomorrow may not come. Today, and what I do with it, is the most important day of my life.

Immediate Answered Prayer

It usually takes a while for me to get an answer to my prayers.

In January 2015, though, Gayle and I were in Atlanta for the weekend, arriving on Friday. Our daughter Anna lived there. Her husband George owned a food delivery business in Marietta. His primary area was Vinings/Buckhead. Our hotel was in Dunwoody, some distance away, so we planned to see them on Saturday. Late Friday afternoon, Gayle wanted to shop at Perimeter Mall, so I wandered around to find somewhere for dinner while she shopped. Season 52 was the first place I checked out. It was hopping, popular with a good vibe, so that's where we went. The place was full, so we took seats at the bar for dinner. After we ordered, the conversation focused on Anna, who had been extremely sick for some time with Crohn's disease. Truth be told, she looked like death warmed over. Her weight loss was alarming, and she was frail and almost skeletal. We were very concerned about her and even expressed to each other our hope that George would hang in there with her. Since their marriage in 2014, her health challenges had been constant.

After the food arrived, Gayle and I bowed our heads for the blessing. I specifically mentioned Anna and George in my prayer. Our backs were turned to the front door since we sat at the bar, but "something" made us look around, and there was George! Though Dunwoody was not his company's normal area of business, the driver who had taken the order called in sick, so George made the run for the food delivery. We told George about my prayer and our concerns. He told us we had nothing to worry about, that he signed for life when he married Anna, and he would never leave. After he left the restaurant to deliver the order, Gayle and I stared at each other, wondering what had just happened. Of all restaurants in the Atlanta area, George appeared at that particular one, at that precise moment, after a prayer.

Later, I found Scriptures to help us sort it out: Daniel 9:20-23; Luke 3:21; Isaiah 65:24; and Jeremiah 33:3. Sometimes, God moves quickly!

Overcoming My Fear of Public Speaking

It started in my junior year of high school. I became deathly afraid of speaking in public. The first time it hit me, I was giving a campaign speech, or trying to, to be an officer on the student council. The lunchroom was packed with students, teachers, and the principal. When I stepped to the podium and looked out at all the faces staring at me, I froze. My legs shook, my voice cracked, I broke out in a sweat, and my mind went blank with only one thought: run! Somehow, I stumbled and bumbled my way through and, full of shame and embarrassment, slinked back to my seat. I think people voted for me out of pity.

It got worse from there, and I avoided any opportunity to talk in front of a group. But when I was in my early twenties and starting out in real estate, I realized that the inability to express myself to groups of people would hold me back professionally. I enrolled in a Dale Carnegie class, meeting the problem head on. One evening, our assignment was to talk about something we were passionate about. On my way to the podium, the instructor handed me a rolled-up newspaper, telling me to hit the podium every time I wanted to emphasize an important point in my speech.

I chose the topic of drinking and driving and all the senseless accidents, pain, and loss this problem caused our country and society. My talk started slowly with a few gentle raps of the paper, but as I got to the part about innocent loss of life, I began to shout and hit the podium with all the force I had. At the end of the talk, I was exhausted, and the newspaper was torn to shreds. I walked to my seat amid a standing ovation. I realized the secret of giving a good talk: take the focus off yourself. It's not about me. It's about a subject I want the audience to know. It's about a subject I am qualified to talk about and even passionate about.

In every talk since that fateful night, I forget about my appearance, my delivery, and my impression of the group, and I focus on communicating in a meaningful, concise, and clear way. It's not about me.

The Bible Verses that Get Me Through

Two Bible verses have helped me survive many tough situations in my life. I don't think there is a hotter place in the summer than Columbia, South Carolina, specifically Fort Jackson. My barracks that summer of 1970 were built in 1917. The first Sunday I was there, we had the opportunity to go to church. I quickly jumped at the chance. Was this because of my Christian upbringing? My dedication to observing the Sabbath? My close relationship with God? None of the above. I went to the church that day for one reason: it was the only air-conditioned building soldiers could access.

As I settled into my comfortable and cool pew, I noticed the order of service focused on two verses: Psalm 37:4—"Delight yourself in the LORD; And He will give you the desires of your heart"; and Psalm 37:8—"Cease from anger and forsake wrath; Do not fret, it leads only to evildoing" (NASB1995). I left church with a determination that no matter the circumstances, I would be joyful and happy in the Lord and would not get mad at anyone or anything. I faced a multitude of people and situations at Fort Jackson as I have throughout my life, and holding on to these two Bible verses has made a tremendous difference in my success. They also deliver something rare in the world today: peace.

My Most Memorable Sale

Recently, I taught our adult Sunday school class a series of lessons on what the Bible says about where we go when we die. The lessons came from Job, Isaiah, Daniel, Matthew, and Revelation. The developing theology was interesting as we moved from doubt to prophecy and on to what Jesus revealed and what we now know. The subject of the afterlife, which sometimes makes us uncomfortable, ended up providing peace and great comfort as the Holy Spirit guided and taught us. One of my references was to a Broadway play.

In 1925, playwright Eugene O'Neill wrote a play that appeared on Broadway: *Lazarus Laughed*. After Jesus raises Lazarus from the dead, the newly alive man embraces Jesus and sisters Mary and Martha, then heads home to Bethany. Once he gets there, people want to know about his experience: "What was it like? What happens when you die?" Lazarus responds, "There is no death, really. There is only life. There is only God. There is only incredible joy. Death is not the way it appears from this side. Death is not an abyss into which we go into chaos. It is, rather, a portal through which we move into everlasting life."[1] I love this response. And to think it was spoken on Broadway in New York City!

In 1931, O'Neill was the nation's most famous playwright. He sought a getaway spot for himself and his wife, actress Carlotta Monterey. As Harold Martin states in his book *This Happy Isle*, Gene was weary and tense after years in France.[2] He and Carlotta got word of a remote island off the coast of Georgia, a "place of peace" called Sea Island. They immediately bought an oceanfront lot on 19th Street and built a spacious "twenty-two room house of Spanish peasant style," calling it Casa Genotta. (As an aside, O'Neill wrote his only comedy on Sea Island, *Ah, Wilderness*.) The island and their house, at Cottage 57 East Agramont Road, provided the refuge they needed from the public. In 1936, the same year O'Neill won the Nobel Prize, they sold the house to the Cluett family, the shirt makers (of Cluett, Peabody & Company). They kept it until 1953, when the Gasque family purchased it.

From 1982 to 2012, I worked for the Sea Island Company. In March 1986, my telephone rang. On the other end was Bud Gasque, asking me to help his family sell Cottage 57. I met them at the house. Eugene O'Neill's study was upstairs, overlooking the ocean. At the rear of the house, this room suggested a ship and a captain's cabin. The views of the Atlantic Ocean were inspiring. What amazed me most is that O'Neill's office, desk, cabinets, and files were in place as if he had just gone down to the Cloister for afternoon tea. Our company listed the house for sale.

As soon as I returned to the office, I called Jim Timmons. Jim and Anita had lived in Montclair, New Jersey, when Jim worked in New York. Eugene O'Neill was Anita's favorite playwright. I had heard her speak warmly of him.

The telephone conversation went something like this:

"Hello, Jim. Al Brown here. I have your house."

"What do you mean?"

"I've just listed Eugene O'Neill's house, Cottage 57."

"We'll take it…how much is it?"

I took Jim and Anita to the house that day. When I opened the front door, and then throughout our tour of the house, Anita broke down in tears. This was truly their dream house, perhaps my most memorable showing in my real estate career spanning fifty-two years.

It's satisfying to find the home of our dreams, especially when it has extra sentimental value because of where it is or who it belonged to. But our number one problem in life is not where to live. It's where to spend eternity. For believers in Christ, that problem is solved.

In O'Neill's play, Lazarus could laugh because he experienced life after death firsthand. One day, we will experience that miracle too. For now, we can laugh by faith and with hope.

[1]Eugene O'Neill, *Lazarus Laughed*, in *Complete Plays 1920–1931* (New York: Library of America, 1988), 537–628.
[2]Harold H. Martin, *This Happy Isle: The Story of Sea Island and the Cloister* (Sea Island Company, 1978).

Told Not to Pray

In the early 1990s, Gayle and I were PTSA (Parent, Teacher, Student Association) co-presidents for Glynn Middle School in Brunswick, Georgia. It was time for the big annual meeting in the school auditorium, attended by hundreds of people. I was asked to do the "devotional" with the plea, or should I say command, not to say a prayer. Wanting to cooperate, I asked if a quote or two would be acceptable. I was given the okay, so when the meeting was called to order and I was asked to offer the devotional, I quoted two of our country's greatest presidents.

George Washington: "…it is the duty of all Nations to acknowledge the providence of Almighty God, to obey his will, to be grateful for his benefits, and humbly to implore his protection and favor."[1]

Abraham Lincoln: "In regard to this Great Book [the Bible], …it is the best gift God has given to man. All the good the Savior gave to the world was communicated through this book."[2]

As I walked back to my seat, I saw a number of smiles and thumbs-up signs.

[1] From "George Washington's Thanksgiving Proclamation," October 3, 1789, *Smithsonian*, https://www.si.edu/spotlight/thanksgiving/proclamation.

[2] From *Collected Works of Abraham Lincoln*, vol. 7 [Nov. 5, 1863–Sept. 12, 1864] (New Brunswick, NJ: Rutgers University Press, 1953).

Worn-out Basketball

One day in the middle 1960s toward the end of my tenth-grade year, I overhead Mama and Daddy talking in the kitchen. Daddy was employed by the city of Elberton, Georgia. Supporting a family of six, he always seemed concerned about finances and whether our family had enough money. Probably for a good reason. Nobody gets rich working for a municipality, especially a small one. Daddy had a deep sense of service in his heart, and he gave his all for the betterment of Elberton. When he died, the flags there flew at half-mast.

My parents' conversation that day was grave. Daddy wondered out loud how he would be able to meet the impending obligations of two children in college (my sister Jean and me). At that moment, when I peered in and saw the furrowed, sweaty brow of my father, I made up my mind to do something to help. But what?

After much thought, I realized what a godsend it would be for me to get a basketball scholarship. I would make Daddy proud! But how would I, in the middle of a football-crazy town in the foothills of northeast Georgia, accomplish a feat so few athletes achieve?

I decided to get as good as I could get and see what happened. I would do my part, let God do the rest, then let the chips fall where they may. The next day, I went to see my high school coach, Chester Webb, and told him my plan. Coach Webb handed me the keys to the gym, gave me a new basketball, and wished me good luck. Then I made a simple plan and commitment: practice hard every day. We lived in the country, so each day I dribbled a mile on the highway and ran a mile in addition to practicing shooting and dribbling drills.

I got pretty good. I was scouted by Georgia and Clemson, who I think left at halftime, but I ended up with a full scholarship to Gainesville College in Gainesville, Georgia—to Daddy's great relief. I took pride in accomplishing my goal.

That basketball, worn and tattered, sits on a shelf in my office as a constant reminder of the results of hard work and determination.

Perseverance (in Bed)

By 1971, Gayle and I had been dating close to five years, and we began to talk about marriage. It was time for me to ask her father for her hand. We picked the perfect summer night. The Atlanta Braves were playing on TV, so that would keep her parents at home for the evening. After dinner, we settled in to watch the game together. But the evening didn't go quite as planned. Gayle's mother went to bed before the game ended, which was fine. But the Braves had to play extra innings, only to lose. Around 11:30 p.m., Gayle's father, Mr. Cleveland, bounced out of his recliner and headed straight for the bedroom, slamming the door in disgust at the loss.

Gayle gave me one of her looks. It's not a good look. It's one of disappointment and disgust. All the husbands out there know what I mean. After ten or fifteen minutes, her response was, "Well, what are you going to do now?" I said, "I'm going in."

With that, I gently knocked on their bedroom door, the lights obviously already turned off.

"Yes?" Mr. Cleveland called out.

"It's me, Al. Can I come in?"

"Yes. Come on in."

As I entered the room, they turned on the bedside lamp, remaining under the covers. I took a seat at the end of the bed, addressed Gayle's father as respectfully as I could, and humbly asked for Gayle's hand in marriage.

I got the approval and the blessing and sort of slinked out of their bedroom as the light went out. Then I said to Gayle in the living room, "He said yes!"

Discovery of a Talent

My grades in elementary school were mostly A's. When I was in high school, in eighth grade, I received my first D in music. I was devastated. As I stood at the teacher's desk getting my grade, my lips quivered with shame, as I knew how disappointed Mama and Daddy would be. The teacher comforted me by saying that not all children are good at music, and some like me simply don't have musical ability. She said she would do her best the rest of the year to try to get me out of the class with a C, but she also advised, "Don't ever take another class in music."

I turned fourteen years old a year later, and one Friday night at a dance at the Recreation Center, I found myself transfixed by the drummer of the band. I watched him and said to myself, "I can do that." The following day, a group of parents took some of us to play baseball at the Rec Center field. We took a break to go to the main building for water. The band from the night before had not taken the instruments home. Two of my friends played the guitar. One picked up the lead guitar, the other picked up the bass guitar, and they started playing. Not seeing any drumsticks, I went to the kitchen drawer and pulled out two butter knives. They worked fine for drumsticks, and the boys looked on, dumbfounded.

As soon as I got home, I went to the woods behind the house, cut two limbs from a sweet gum tree, and carved out two drumsticks. Next, I fetched three cardboard boxes that carried Mama's groceries. As cymbals, I used a bottle for one and a sheet of tin foil for the other. I set things up in the basement right beside the record player.

The next day, brimming with confidence at the unexpected discovery of my new "gift," I proudly proclaimed to Daddy that I could play the drums. Of course, Daddy gave me some pushback, but I adamantly held to my position and said how much I wanted a set of drums. Daddy didn't see much risk in his reply: "Tell you what, son. Show me you can play the drums and I'll pay half." The set I wanted cost $129.95. That was a lot of money to us almost sixty years ago.

Rock and roll was my style then, but Frank Sinatra came out with a song Daddy liked: "Strangers in the Night." I purchased a .45 of that record and learned the drum parts by ear. I never learned to read one bit of music. The day came when I invited Daddy to the basement to show him what I could do. When the song finished, Daddy said, "Well, I'll be. You can play the drums. Save up half and I'll match it."

It was another year before I bought my first set of Ludwigs. I played in several bands, plus the local production of *The Sound of Music*. I have played in numerous church concerts with orchestras, and every Sunday I play in church.

Baker Thomas, one of our previous ministers of music at First Baptist Church on St. Simons Island, Georgia, told me I have an expert's ability at tonal memory or aural recall. It comes to me as a natural gift from God, and I give God the glory and honor.

The carved drumsticks from 1964 are proudly displayed on a shelf in my office. And I never went against my teacher's advice: no music class for me.

Always Trust a Woman's Intuition

People ask Gayle and me how we ended up on St. Simons Island, Georgia, a small island about seventy-five miles north of Jacksonville, Florida. Gayle always lights up when someone asks because the answer makes her look so good!

We both grew up in Elberton, a small town in the foothills of northeast Georgia. We loved growing up there and had idyllic upbringings. We married in March 1972, while I had another quarter of school to finish at the University of Georgia. Gayle was teaching school in Hartwell, Georgia. I was driving to Athens each day for morning classes, surveying with Uncle Max in the afternoons, and playing drums with a country band on the weekends. My major at Georgia was real estate, and I even got my sales license in fall 1971, though my primary interest was real estate finance.

After graduating in June 1971, I soon discovered that the job market was tight for someone in my chosen field. While all my friends were hired, I practically wore out a pair of shoes looking for a job in Atlanta, Augusta, Athens, and Macon, as well as in Columbia and Greenville, South Carolina. I sent my resume all over the southeastern US, all the way to Miami.

Gayle kept bringing up where she thought we should live: St. Simons Island, Georgia. I had never been there or heard of it and had to get out a map to find it. When I saw it, I ridiculed her for thinking a place that small could offer anything for me to do, given all the big places I had searched.

One day, I had enough of her persistence. We lived in a two-bedroom mobile home at the time, and I invited her to the sofa by the phone, telling her to watch and listen. I dialed for directory assistance to Brunswick, Georgia, asking for the name of a bank and a savings and loan. The bank was First National Bank of Brunswick. I was twenty-one years old at the time, more than a little frustrated at being unemployed. To the receptionist who answered the phone, I ordered, "The president of the bank, please." "Yes, sir," she replied. The bank president answered immediately, identifying himself as Myd Harris.

"Mr. Harris, this is Al Brown from Elberton, Georgia."

"Al Brown! How in the world are you doing?" he exclaimed like I was his long-lost friend.

"I'm fine, Mr. Harris, but I'm looking for a job in real estate finance. I have a degree in real estate from the University of Georgia, I have my real estate license, and somehow, I've already made a sale. But you know what? I know absolutely nothing about real estate, and I'm not interested in driving 275 miles to hear you say you are looking for someone with experience."

There was a long pause. Then Mr. Harris finally spoke. "Just last Thursday, we had a management meeting to discuss adding to our mortgage loan department. Can you come down next week?"

After hanging up the phone, I looked across the room at Gayle and sheepishly said, "I'll never doubt you again." This has served me well in a fifty-two-year marriage to this strong-willed, determined woman who has low tolerance for failure.

The following week, I interviewed and got the job. As we prepared to move to the coast of Georgia, I vividly remember going to close our bank account in Elberton, all $301 of it. That was what we had. We rented the smallest U-Haul trailer available and started our new life together on a piece of God's paradise, St. Simons Island, Georgia. We've been here for fifty-two years. I think we'll stay. All thanks to a woman's intuition and, no doubt, the Lord's guidance.

The Bible Verse that Changed My Life

I don't believe anything is an accident if it leads us to something good. One day I stumbled over a verse "by accident"—John 14:23.

Jesus says, "If anyone loves Me, he will keep My word; and my Father will love him, and We will come to him and make our abode with him" (NASB1995). At first, the verse gave me great comfort. The Maker of the universe and his son Jesus would make their abode with me! Then, the verse terrified me. Even though I was thirty-three years old and had grown up in the church, I realized I didn't really know God's word, the Bible. That day, I decided to get serious about knowing God's word, and I made a commitment to read and study it daily. That day and that verse changed my life.

A Seven-year-old Teaches Me How to Coach

My first year of coaching girls' softball was going well. We were 8-0 and headed into the final stretch of the season. I was considered a fantastic coach, patient and kind, even though I practiced the girls on Saturdays in addition to weekday practices. We were playing the ninth game of the season, and it came down to the last inning. We lost a very close game by one run.

As the winning players charged the field, I remained on the bench, pouring over the line-up card: maybe if I had moved Jordan up to hit third rather than second…perhaps I should have put Sara in another slot…decisions, decisions!

Suddenly a sweet voice next to me spoke. "Coach, is the game over yet?" I answered, "Yes." She gently took my hand and said, "Coach, can we go get our snow cone now?" I smiled, closed my notebook of strategy, and said, "That's a great idea."

That one moment changed my philosophy about coaching. From then on, it was about having fun. In fact, my pre-game speech from that day on was, "Okay, ladies, let's get this game over with so we can go get our snow cones."

Playing loose as a goose with no pressure, my teams won far more than they lost.

In the game of life, God doesn't care about winning. He wants a witness, and He wants us to have fun.

A Weird Way to Cope

I admit I have idiosyncrasies, but they help get me through challenging times.

In 2006, I was replaced as head of the real estate department at Sea Island Company. My job performance was superb, but I began to question some of the company's business plan strategies. My boss claimed that I no longer believed in his vision for the future of the company, so he replaced me. Basically, in sports lingo, I got benched.

In 2008, we could hear the distant drums of financial trouble on the horizon. Rumors of bankruptcy continued through 2009, and in 2010, Sea Island Company filed for Chapter 11, later selling in December 2010. During the process, I took a 60 percent salary cut and endured the heart-breaking task of being a part of terminating more than 500 wonderful employees. My future pension got cut by 50 percent, and my net worth fell by 84 percent as my stock appreciation rights, a major part of my financial security, went to zero. It was a sad night when I had to go home and tell Gayle this news.

Now the "weird" part. Some people turn to drugs, alcohol, or pills when faced with the need to get away. I turned to bass fishing and the Lord. Fishing became my diversion. From October 15, 2008, until June 11, 2010, I fished at least a little every single day. 609 straight days of wetting a hook. Living on a freshwater lake on St. Simons Island, Georgia, certainly helped. I kept a log of the days and places. In fact, I submitted it to the Guinness Book of World Records in London. They considered it, then said, "Nah." Oh, well. I survived and came through stronger than ever.

When you face tough times and have to do something to cope, throw yourselves into something fun, clean, and legal, even if it seems weird. God will bless you for it, just like He blessed me.

Career Decisions

In 1971, as a junior majoring in real estate at the University of Georgia, I got my real estate license. I had no interest or aptitude in sales but thought the experience of getting my license would be educational. I hung it in the real estate office of George Goss Real Estate in Elberton, Georgia. I did a little work there and somehow actually made a sale. But sales, I thought at the time, was not a field for me. Mr. Goss agreed as he took Daddy aside to say, "Allen, you need to get Al out of sales. This is definitely not the field for him." When Daddy told me that later, I think it fired me up a little because I love a challenge. Tell me I can't do something, then stand by and watch!

My approach to sales was different. I had no appetite for the hard-sell, aggressive approach. That was not my style. I analyzed my strengths: a good listener, excellent analytical skills, empathy, calm, problem solver, deliberate demeanor, and the attitude of telling the truth about every property in order to let the customer make a final decision after knowing the facts. In short, I build trust. This formula works. In my career, I have a residential sales volume exceeding $1.65 billion. Thank you, God, for my gifts and for showing me how to use them.

Papa, the Sheep Farmer

My paternal grandfather was Herman Judson Brown, born in 1895 in Elberton, Georgia. He played baseball for the University of Georgia in 1912–1913. He returned to Elberton after serving in the Army to live on a farm, where he earned a living as a sheep farmer and cotton buyer. I used to fish a lot with Papa on the farm pond. He taught me how to chew tobacco at age fourteen, a secret we kept from my parents. It was Bohannon's Favorite, a plug tobacco. That company probably went out of business when Papa died.

Papa taught me some amazing things about the behavior of sheep. When I read references in the Bible about sheep, I have already observed them on the farm. Indeed, they know the voice of their master. At a public market, with two different herds of sheep corralled in a pen, I watched Papa call his sheep as he opened the pen door, and only his sheep marched out, one by one.

Sheep are helpless animals with no way to defend themselves. When wild dogs come into the pasture, a sheep will stand there and be attacked by the dogs, literally eaten to death. Papa used to call Daddy and tell him to bring the boys and your guns because "the wild dogs are back."

God is referred to as the caring, protecting Shepherd, most famously in the 23rd Psalm. God's "sheep" are followers, trusting in his guidance. We, too, like Papa's sheep, need a Protector we can call on. If we know our Shepherd and his voice, He will answer us. Remember that as you face spiritual attacks and also when you call out for help and/or guidance.

PART 2
Bible Book Summaries

The Bible is holy yet mysterious. In its simplest form, the Old Testament is about a nation, Israel. The New Testament is about a Man, Jesus. The nation was formed to bring forth the Man, whose purpose is to redeem the world. In the Bible, God reveals Himself to us.

I will offer a succinct summary of the heart of each Bible book that unlocks the mystery for me. These are a father's reflections, notes from my Bible (New American Standard Bible, *The Open Bible* edition) that relate to personal experiences, research, and teaching an adult Sunday school class using the Smyth & Helwys *Formations* Teaching Guide and *Formations* Commentary, the Life Application Study Bible, and *Halley's Bible Handbook*—always taught and led by the Holy Spirit.

I hope my notes inspire you to further study through your personal Bible reading, commentaries, and other ways to learn about Scripture.

The Old Testament

The books of the Old Testament are arranged in a logical order:
- seventeen historical books—Genesis to Esther
- five poetical books—Job to Song of Solomon
- and seventeen prophetical books—Isaiah to Malachi.

As you study, know that the books of the Bible are not arranged in chronological order, and their dates of writing are not always known with certainty. The Old Testament books are grouped by category: historical, poetical, prophetical. Therefore, some of the books have overlapping time periods.

GENESIS
(FIRST BOOK OF MOSES)

Genesis is about the creation of everything: the heavens, the earth, animals, man, woman. It is also about humankind's fall and the consequences and seriousness of sin. The book contains the stories of Noah and the flood and the founding of the Hebrew nation.

Moses wrote Genesis from ancient documents, guided by God. Creation did not happen by accident. God had a plan, a promise, and a land. And God had a love for His children in creating man and woman, neither exalted and neither depreciated. The creation of humans established the sanctity and basis of the origin of family: man and woman.

Chapters 1–11 set the stage and hold the key to our understanding of the entire Bible, both Old Testament and New Testament. God reveals Himself as Creator, our loving Father, the Provider, and a just Judge. Satan introduces sin into God's perfect creation. A holy God is unable to tolerate sin, and there are consequences for sin. Even with those consequences, God chose Noah and Abraham to bless the world through the nation of Israel, ultimately leading to Jesus Christ.

Written in 1450–1410 BC to the people of Israel, Genesis still reveals God's personality and character to readers today.

EXODUS
(SECOND BOOK OF MOSES)

The exodus is the central event in the Old Testament. We can divide the book of Exodus into two sections. Chapters 1–18 are filled with action. The Israelites are enslaved in Egypt. Moses is born, and he grows up and meets God at the burning bush. Instructed by God, he confronts Pharaoh, and God sends ten plagues to convince the Egyptians to let God's people go. God leads the Hebrew people across the Red Sea and toward the promised land in Canaan. The Israelites spend forty years in the wilderness before entering the promised land.

Chapters 19–40 are filled with instruction, including the Ten Commandments in chapter 20. God tells the people what it means to live in covenant with the Lord. Moses wrote this book about the birth of the Hebrew nation during the same period he wrote Genesis, 1450–1410 BC. God chose Moses, even though he wasn't perfect. God brought the enslaved people out of Egypt to begin the story of salvation.

LEVITICUS
(THIRD BOOK OF MOSES)

Without Leviticus, especially chapter 16 about holiness and sacrifice and chapter 26 about the blessings of obedience and the penalties for disobedience, Christians could never fully understand the powerful message of the cross, where Jesus became the sacrificial Lamb of God, slain for us. A final sacrifice.

The events in the book took place between 1445 and 1444 BC.

Chapters 1–16 include rituals and ceremonial topics, religious sacrifices, and sacred feasts.

Chapters 17–27 are about moral and social issues for all Israelites and also rules for priests. Some of the Bible is cultural. Some ancient customs were unique to their time and place (like Sabbath laws, dietary observances, slavery, women's status, and marital laws).

Leviticus 26 is one of the great chapters of the Bible. We are reminded of God's promises if we obey but warned about consequences of disobeying.

NUMBERS
(FOURTH BOOK OF MOSES)

Written 1450–1410 BC, Numbers details the Israelites' forty years in the desert. They learn how to function as a camp. Moses wrote this book to the people of Israel to tell the story of how they prepared to enter the promised land of Canaan, how they sinned and were punished, and how they prepared to try again. Tragedy can lead to transformation and positive change.

Numbers 14:22-24 are key verses. God says the people thought occupying the promised land was all about them. They missed the point: it was really all about God.

DEUTERONOMY
(FIFTH BOOK OF MOSES)

Jesus often quoted verses from Deuteronomy. The book contains Moses's farewell address and a solemn warning. He wrote most of it around 1407 BC (Joshua wrote the end) to remind the Jewish people what God had done for them and to urge them to rededicate their lives to serve and obey God.

The passages emphasize the importance of a central place of worship. For the central theme, see Deuteronomy 6:4-9, 12-14; 7:9-11.

JOSHUA

Moses dies, and the mantle of leadership passes from him to Joshua. Joshua takes over God's higher assignment at the time: leading God's people—more than two million of them—into the promised land after forty years of wilderness wandering. The book, written by Joshua and a high priest around 1367–1377 BC, details the conquest and settlement of Canaan.

Key verses include Joshua 1:7-9; 24:14-15, where the people are urged to have courage and serve the Lord.

JUDGES

The book of Judges, written by an anonymous author (possibly Samuel) around 1400–1100 BC, details 1,300 years of oppression and then the deliverance of the Hebrew nation. The people of Israel lapse into serving idols after Joshua's death. They enter a pattern of falling away from the worship of God and turning to the Canaanite fertility gods. God punishes them with military defeat and subjection. They pray to God, and God raises up a judge to save them. A period of peace follows. The pattern repeats several times.

God is supposed to be the direct Ruler of Israel. The people do not take God seriously, so God uses evil people to punish them.

Judges 17:6 is a key verse. The Israelites neglected worship of God; wanted a peaceful coexistence with the Canaanites at any cost; and became envious of Canaanite prosperity. Credit was given to the idol Baal for the fertility of the land.

RUTH

Written at an unknown time by an anonymous author, Ruth is a beautiful love story that occurs during a dark time in Israel's history. People lived to please themselves instead of God. Ruth, not an Israelite but a Moabite woman, sets the standard for spiritual character.

Ruth 1:16 is a key verse in which Ruth promises to stay true to her mother-in-law Naomi no matter what happens.

1 SAMUEL

Samuel was Israel's last judge before the nation went from a theocracy to a monarchy. The date for the writing of 1 and 2 Samuel is not known for certain. Portions of 1 Samuel and all of 2 Samuel were written after Samuel's death. The events of 1 Samuel occurred around 1100–1050 BC. The book records the life of Samuel, the reign and decline of Saul (the first king of Israel), and God's choice of David, Israel's greatest king, in spite of his sins.

The story of David and Goliath in chapter 17 is a highlight.

The basic message of both 1–2 Samuel is that God rules in the lives of people and nations. God is working towards his goal of preparing the people for the coming Messiah.

2 SAMUEL

The events of 2 Samuel occurred in approximately 1010–970 BC. It was probably written shortly after King David's reign ended in 970 BC. Second Samuel records the reign of King David, including the story of David's great sin in chapter 11.

A continued theme is that God is working the divine purpose through all events of Israel's history, preparing a people through whom a Savior will come.

1 KINGS

The book of 1 Kings, written anonymously (but perhaps by Jeremiah or a group of prophets) and with a time period of 970–852 BC, opens with the Hebrew nation in its glory, while 2 Kings closes with the nation in ruins. God's blessings flowed to those who obeyed His commandments, and judgment fell on the disobedient.

God's messengers were prophets sent to remind the people of God's covenant and its provisions. The people refused to separate and distinguish themselves from the religious practices of surrounding nations. The kingdom divides at chapter 12. Various kings are rated as good or bad. The worst king, Ahab, is convinced by Jezebel (1 Kings 17:29-33) that the God of Moses, Joshua, Samuel, and David is out of date and old-fashioned.

One theme is that a nation's leadership impacts the spiritual commitment of its people. Handling wealth, power, and praise can be challenging.

2 KINGS

In the Hebrew Old Testament, 1 and 2 Kings were one book. Though the writer is unknown, scholars speculate that it may have been Jeremiah or a group of prophets.

The book's time period is 852–560 BC, which covers the last 130 years of the northern kingdom of Israel and the last 250 years of the southern kingdom of Judah.

To learn why Israel fell, read 2 Kings 17:7-23. Overall, the Hebrew people had moved farther and farther away from their history, heritage, and core beliefs. It was hard to stop this harmful trend.

1 CHRONICLES

First Chronicles retells the story of the first twelve books of the Bible. Repetition equals importance; some of it is dry reading, but there are jewels.

The book, written by Ezra in approximately 430 BC primarily to record events that occurred in 1000–960 BC, is the story of Israel from creation to the death of David.

The book's purpose is to unify God's people, emphasize the importance of worship, and teach that genuine worship ought to be the center of a person's life.

2 CHRONICLES

Written by Ezra in approximately 430 BC and recording events in 970–586 BC, 2 Chronicles records the history of the southern kingdom by Judah.

The kingdom of Israel split approximately 930 BC, forming two new kingdoms: the northern kingdom of Israel (ten tribes) with Samaria as the capital and the southern kingdom of Judah (two tribes) with Jerusalem as the capital. Israel fell to the Assyrians 721/722 BC. Judah fell to the Babylonians 586 BC.

Key verses in the book are 2 Chronicles 7:14, God's promise, and 16:9, God's promise and warning.

EZRA

The priest and scribe Ezra wrote this book around 450 BC, recording events from 538–450 BC about the exiles' return from captivity and rebuilding of the temple. The leaders of the Persian Empire permitted the Jews to return to their homeland, fulfilling God's promises.

Key verses include Ezra 3:2, 8, about focusing on worship of God and beginning work on the new temple.

(Note: Ezra, Nehemiah, and Esther cover about 100 years and form the closing section of the Old Testament story in the historical books.)

NEHEMIAH

Nehemiah, cup bearer to the Persian king and later appointed governor in Judah, wrote this book about rebuilding the walls of Jerusalem and restoring spiritual practices in the worship of God. He covers the time period from 445 to about 420 BC.

For key verses, see Nehemiah 6:15-16, which detail the completion of the temple wall and point the surrounding people to God's work.

ESTHER

An anonymous author (possibly Mordecai) wrote Esther, a book about Jewish heritage containing drama, power, romance, and intrigue.

In this portrait of a courageous leader, Esther becomes queen in 478 BC. She saves the Jews from massacre in 473 BC.

The book's main themes are to lead yourself first, have a mission that matters, be ethical, think big, be open to change, create change, be sensitive, take risks, make decisions, use power wisely, be courageous, and communicate. Celebrate the defeat of evil, and remember that God sometimes works through ordinary people "for such a time as this" (Esther 4:14).

JOB

The book of Job, written anonymously at an unknown time, ponders the question, "Why do the righteous suffer?" We can explain some suffering, but sometimes it just doesn't make sense. Job gets sarcastic in chapter 12, has a "leave me alone" attitude in chapter 13, becomes doubtful in chapter 14, and makes a magnificent recovery in Job 19:24-25. His mistake was passing judgment on God to justify his own worldview. Job obtains a new understanding of God through his suffering. God never deserts us. We must let God be God. As Christians, we know that God came to earth and suffered, too.

PSALMS

The purpose of Psalms is to provide poetry for the expression of praise, worship, and confession. Psalms is about trust, not a promise of deliverance from every adversity. May we learn to trust God in every circumstance. If you have trouble sleeping, I recommend memorizing passages from Psalms. They can bring peace and restore your rest.

Various people wrote the Psalms. It is thought that David wrote seventy-five of them; Asaph twelve; the sons of Korah nine; Solomon two; Moses, Heman, and Ethan forty-nine; and three are anonymous.

They were composed between the time of Moses (approximately 1440 BC) and the time of the Babylon captivity (586 BC).

PROVERBS

Likely written by King Solomon early in his reign (970–931 BC), Proverbs is a collection of sayings about the practical things of everyday life. The purpose is to teach readers how to attain wisdom, discipline, and prudence and to do what is right, just, and fair. This healing book defines wisdom as knowledge guided by understanding.

Proverbs 1:7 is a key verse pointing to the Lord as the source of wisdom.

ECCLESIASTES

Ecclesiastes, traditionally thought to be written by Solomon around 935 BC, is possibly the strangest book in the Bible. Solomon looks back on his life and gives reflections of a man who tried to find meaning in life apart from God. We get the impression that Solomon was not a happy man. A good point to remember is that all scripture is not created equal; not all of Solomon's ideas are God's ideas.

A key verse is Ecclesiastes 12:13, which sums up what Solomon learned.

THE SONG OF SOLOMON

Another supposed writing of Solomon around 973 BC, the purpose of this book is to tell about the love between a bridegroom and his bride and the joys of wedded life and love. While many readers avoid this Bible book because it is sensual and sexy, and some insist it is an allegory, it contains a positive and exciting message about real relationships. Solomon, the wisest man in the world, is smitten by yet another woman.

Two lovers describe each other and the intimate feelings they share, celebrating the anticipation and joy of sex. God meant for sex to be a blessing. The story of the couple's romance emphasizes that we should give our partners our full attention.

ISAIAH

The first of the prophetical writings in the Bible, Isaiah is the most quoted book in the New Testament. Isaiah was a prophet of the southern kingdom of Judah who wrote around 739 to 681 BC.

The events in chapters 1–39 occurred during Isaiah's ministry around 700 BC when the Assyrian Empire was in power. The message is generally one of judgment, though chapter 35 covers the future return of the exiles, visions of the last days, and a glimpse of the glory of our heavenly home with God. Chapter 39 refers to the Babylonian captivity.

Chapters 40–66 include the Persians' overthrow of Babylon as predicted by Isaiah. In chapter 40, the prophet begins to comfort Judah instead of warning them of judgment. He begins to speak of events that will occur after their captivity.

The book contains so much prophecy that Isaiah is known as "The Messianic Prophet." He ends on a high note, speaking of Jerusalem's future.

Isaiah 53:5 is a key verse for Christians, who apply this prophecy to Jesus Christ.

JEREMIAH

The prophet Jeremiah, who lived about 100 years after Isaiah in the time period 627–586 BC, wrote about God's final effort to save Jerusalem. Isaiah had saved Jerusalem from Assyria. Jeremiah tried to save Jerusalem from Babylon but failed. Rather than becoming a cynic after the fall of Jerusalem, however, he had a great vision of the future.

Jeremiah urged God's people to turn back to God. He was a failure in man's eyes but very successful in God's eyes.

Jeremiah 29:11-14 and 31:31-34 offer the good news of the book.

LAMENTATIONS

The book of Lamentations is a mourning speech by the prophet Jeremiah, who wrote soon after the fall of Jerusalem in 586 BC. The people had been killed, tortured, or taken captive by the Babylonians and the city destroyed. Lamentations includes bitterness, lashing out, and some blaming of God. In Lamentations 3:59, the writer appeals to God, and the book ends with a prayer for mercy.

EZEKIEL

This book was written around 517 BC by Ezekiel, the prophet of the Babylonian captivity who lived with hardship and persecution. The first twenty-four chapters focus on God's judgment against Israel's unfaithfulness. Then the tone changes to comfort, hope, cleansing, and healing.

Chapters 25–32 contain judgment against seven foreign nations. Chapters 33–39, after the fall of Jerusalem, offer prophecy, encouragement, and hope for a new relationship with God. Chapters 40–48 include visions of a restored temple and nations.

Key verses are Ezekiel 36:24-28, where God promises the people "a new heart" and "a new spirit."

DANIEL

Written around 536 BC, likely by the prophet Daniel, this book is to the Old Testament what Revelation is to the New Testament. From chapters

1–6, the book is generally historical, recording events that occurred from about 605–536 BC.

Chapters 7–12 contain prophecy, including a prediction of the Messiah (9:24-25) and the first clear reference to the resurrection (12:2).

Daniel was taken captive and deported to Babylon in 605 BC. He served in the government there for about seventy years. His writing helped the Jews hold on to their faith in hard times and under persecution. Daniel honored God, and God honored Daniel. Daniel and his friends stayed faithful.

HOSEA

Possibly among the most disturbing Bible books, Hosea is about repentance and includes important symbolism. God commands the prophet Hosea to take a wife of harlotry. She is unfaithful to him, but Hosea pursues her to bring her back.

Written by Hosea around 715 BC recording events from around 753–715 BC, the book illustrates God's love for sinful people and God's willingness to forgive and restore relationships for those who repent.

JOEL

This short and powerful book of coming judgment offers a warning but is also filled with hope. We can find strength in this troublesome book.

The prophet Joel probably wrote this between 835–796 BC to a prosperous and complacent people of Judah. They took God for granted. For all God's blessings, we must sincerely and consistently follow him. Joel 2:28-32 contains a promise of an outpouring of God's spirit.

AMOS

Amos, first a shepherd and then a prophet of the southern kingdom of Judah, likely wrote this between 760–750 BC. God called him away from his home to deliver a message to Israel, the northern kingdom.

The message was a pronouncement of judgment upon Israel for their idolatry, complacency, and neglect to care for the poor. They lost their ability to recognize sin. At some point, God's wrath and judgment always come forth.

OBADIAH

Possibly written 855–840 or 627–586 BC, Obadiah is the shortest book in the Old Testament. Doom is pronounced on the Edomites, the Jews' bitter enemies. They refused passage to Moses (Numbers 20:14-21) and rejoiced when Jerusalem fell. This is not an uplifting book, but it shows what God does to those who harm his people. The Edomites disappeared from history after Jerusalem was destroyed in AD 70.

JONAH

Jonah wrote his story in approximately 785–760 BC to show God's grace and message of salvation to all people. With its uncomplicated and fast-moving plot, some call the book of Jonah a missionary text. God tells Jonah to minister to the Ninevites. Jonah hates the Ninevites. God loves them. The Ninevites repent, and God forgives them. Jonah must learn a hard lesson in an unusual way.

Nineveh (modern-day Iraq) was the capital of the Assyrian Empire. The city was later destroyed in 612 BC.

MICAH

Written by the prophet Micah in approximately 742–687 BC, this address to the northern and southern kingdoms warns God's people that judgment is coming but also offers a pardon and forgiveness to those who repent.

Micah looks beyond a dark period to a glorious future filled with hope and promise. He predicts the fall of Jerusalem in 3:9-12, makes a prediction about Babylon in 4:10 when the Assyrians are in power, and mentions Bethlehem as the Messiah's birthplace in chapter 5 (the only mention in the Old Testament). Micah foretells what we know as the story of Jesus: the exact time of Jesus's birth in Bethlehem to a virgin, his upbringing in Nazareth, his forerunner (John the Baptist), his working of miracles, his way of teaching in parables, his rejection, his death, and his resurrection, which would introduce the era of the Holy Spirit.

The so-called "Micah Manifesto" is at 6:8, presenting God's purpose for people.

NAHUM

Writing probably between 663–612 BC, the prophet Nahum pronounced God's judgment and destruction of Nineveh, the capital of Assyria, and comforted Judah with this prophecy.

HABAKKUK

Between 612 and 589 BC, the prophet Habakkuk, a true optimist, wrote to show that God is still in control of the world even though it appears that evil is winning. Babylon was becoming the dominant world power, and Judah would soon experience its destructive forces. Habakkuk can't understand why God would allow a wicked nation to destroy God's own nation. We are taught to look for God's purpose, not our own.

ZEPHANIAH

Probably around 640–621 BC, the prophet Zephaniah wrote that God's punishment for sin is on the way. He wanted to warn the people of Judah to shake them out of their complacency and urge their return to God. The book starts with doom and gloom but has a happy, hopeful ending. God was not finished with Israel. The themes are judgment and rejoicing.

HAGGAI

The basic message of the prophet Haggai is to complete the job of rebuilding the temple. Writing in 520 BC, he tells the people to make it a priority.

In a key verse, 1:4, Haggai points out the discrepancy between the people's dwellings and God's dwelling.

ZECHARIAH

Zechariah, both priest and prophet, wrote specific predictions about the coming of the Messiah and about future events to give hope to God's people. He also prophesied against enemy nations.

The exiles had returned from captivity in Babylon and desperately needed hope. Chapters 1–8 were written approximately 520–518 BC, and chapters 9–14 were written around 480 BC. See key verses Zechariah 4:6; 9:9-10, which remind readers of God's power.

MALACHI

The prophet Malachi records the final Old Testament message to a disobedient nation. They had been home from Babylon for about 100 years. The priests were lax and degenerate, and the people were discouraged and cynical. They all needed to restore their relationship with God and get serious about worship. Written around 430 BC, Malachi's prophecy answers some questions and tries to make sense of it all.

In a key verse, Malachi 4:2, the prophet points to the way of righteousness and healing.

The New Testament

While the Old Testament is essentially about the forming of a nation, the New Testament is about a Man. The nation had to be founded and formed by God in order to bring forth the Man, Jesus.

MATTHEW

Prior to Jesus's call on his life, Matthew was a tax collector for the Romans.

Around AD 60–65, Matthew wrote this Gospel for the church in Jerusalem, giving special emphasis to Jesus the Messiah as foretold by Old Testament prophets. Jewish civilization was built around the scriptures, so Matthew repeatedly quotes the Old Testament. He also draws a link between Abraham, father of the Jewish nations; David, Israel's greatest king; and Jesus, the Messiah. (See the genealogy of Jesus Christ in chapter 1.)

MARK

Mark, a companion of Paul and Peter, wrote this as the first Gospel (AD 55–65).

He wrote for the Romans, who cared deeply about power, government, and strength. That may be why Mark emphasizes the superhuman power of Jesus. More miracles are recorded in Mark than in any other Gospel. The focus is more on Jesus's deeds than his words. The action is fast paced.

LUKE

The physician Luke, a companion of Paul, is the only known Gentile author in the New Testament.

He wrote around AD 60 specifically for the Gentiles or Greeks. Greek civilization represented culture, philosophy, wisdom, reason, beauty, and education, so Luke appeals to the cultured, orderly, philosophic Greek mind with special emphasis on the humanity of Jesus: his kindness to the weak, the suffering, and the outcast. Dr. Luke also gives a prominent place to women in his writing.

JOHN

John, a fisherman, was a disciple of John the Baptist and Jesus. He wrote this Gospel in approximately AD 85–90 to new Christians, telling a story of Jesus to proclaim him as the Son of God and the key to eternal life. The book is a series of snapshots that share Jesus's life. There are no parables, and John gives no accounts of Jesus's baptism, temptation, the specifics of his birth, or the exorcisms he performed. He offers only a small reference to the Lord's Supper. More than half the book deals with the last week of Jesus's life.

John is recognized as "beloved," the disciple closest to Jesus. He was possibly Jesus's best friend on earth. He states his purpose in writing at John 20:31.

ACTS

Written by Luke (the Gospel author) around AD 60–61 or 63–70, this book is about the formation and spread of the church. The Holy Spirit led the church, just as Jesus had promised. Acts focuses on two of the apostles, Peter and Paul, with most of the book highlighting Paul.

The theme is found in a key verse, Acts 1:8, in which Jesus gives His followers their mission.

ROMANS

Around AD 53–58, Paul wrote to the Romans to let them know he planned to visit them and to give them a sampling of his message. The letter to the Romans is a complete explanation of Paul's understanding of the gospel. Romans 1:16-17 and 10:9 condense his main themes.

The longest and most complex of Paul's letters, Romans is complex and does not offer a "feel-good" theology.

Many Christians believe that Paul lays out God's plan of salvation: In Old Testament times, to impress upon people the seriousness of sin, God decreed that in addition to repentance, contrition, and confession, forgiveness of sin required the shedding of blood. God allowed the sacrifice of an innocent animal in the place of the sinner. Later, God sent a final blood sacrifice in the form of a human, God's son Jesus Christ. Jesus lived a perfect life, was convicted in a mockery of a trial, and was killed on the cross at Calvary outside Jerusalem's walls, becoming the Lamb of God. On the third day, just as the prophets and Jesus promised, God raised Jesus from the grave, overcoming death for him and for us; defeating the evil one for him and for us; and breaking the power of sin for anyone who believes and receives this precious, immortal gift, enabling us to spend eternity with God's in His kingdom and in His presence.

1 CORINTHIANS

Paul wrote this strong, straightforward letter around AD 55 to address problems in the Corinthian church like immorality, factions, lawsuits, meat offered to idols, false apostles, abuses of the Lord's Supper, marriage, and the role of women in the church. Some people denied the resurrection, and Paul was probably the first New Testament writer to record what had been preached about the resurrection.

Key verses are 1:10-11 and 1:23, where Paul urges his readers to have the mind of Christ and to understand that he preaches Christ crucified.

2 CORINTHIANS

Some leaders in the Corinthian church questioned Paul's authority and whether or not he was a genuine apostle, so he wrote this letter between AD 55–57 to affirm his place as a messenger of the gospel.

GALATIANS

Paul wrote this letter to believers in Galatia around AD 49–53 to refute the teaching that Gentile believers must obey Jewish laws to be saved. In 5:1, he expresses a key tenet of Christianity: that Christ sets us free.

This letter is one of the clearest explanations of the gospel. Priest and theologian Martin Luther rediscovered salvation as he studied Galatians, which led him to overturn the widespread understanding of "earning" salvation, a view that dominated the Roman Catholic Church in the early 1500s. The ideas in Galatians formed the basis for the Protestant Reformation.[1]

EPHESIANS

Paul wrote this letter from a Roman prison in approximately AD 60. His themes are reconciliation and the unity of the church.

Ephesians offers an overall view of God's purpose to redeem us. This was God's plan before the foundation of the world.

Read Paul's beautiful prayer for the Ephesians at 3:14-21.

PHILIPPIANS

Written around AD 61 from Rome or possibly Ephesus while Paul was in prison there, this is nonetheless a letter of joy. Such joy despite circumstances comes from Jesus alone.

This letter may be the most personal of Paul's writings. Chapter 4 is especially uplifting. In Ephesians 1:12, Paul affirms that even his hard times are for spreading the gospel.

COLOSSIANS

Paul wrote to the Colossian believers from prison in Rome around AD 60–62. He wrote to combat errors in the church about the deity of Christ and the sufficiency of Christ. The church was still being formed, so it was important to know the truth about these things.

In Colossians 1:22, Paul reminds readers what Jesus did for them in His death on the cross.

Paul's goal was to be a missionary in Spain. Instead, he ended up in prison; because of that, he started writing, and now we have the books of Ephesian, Philippians, Colossians, and Philemon.

1 THESSALONIANS

Written around AD 51, Paul's first letter to the Thessalonians is the second oldest document in the New Testament and probably his earliest surviving letter.

He wrote to encourage the new believers in the Thessalonian church and to settle some of their questions, especially about the Lord's second coming.

First Thessalonians 5:16-18 gives a succinct list of guidance for the Christian life.

2 THESSALONIANS

Paul wrote this letter as a follow-up around AD 51–52 to address confusion about the second coming of Christ.

1 TIMOTHY

Paul wrote this letter to Timothy, his "child in the faith," between his two Roman imprisonments (around AD 61/62–64) to offer encouragement and instruction to this young leader in Ephesus.

In 4:12, Paul sums up his advice to young Timothy.

Note that there are cultural differences to consider when reading the Bible. Always ask yourself, "How does this compare with the teaching of Jesus?"

2 TIMOTHY

This letter is Paul's final word from a Roman prison in AD 66 or 67 as he awaits execution the following year. He gives encouragement and final instructions to Timothy, pastor of the church in Ephesus.

TITUS

Paul wrote to Titus, one of the early Christian converts, in approximately AD 64 or 65. He gives advice on supervising the churches on the island of Crete.

PHILEMON

Around AD 60, Paul wrote this letter, again from prison, to address the challenge of forgiveness. His goal was to convince Philemon, a wealthy member of the Colossian church, to forgive a runaway slave named Onesimus.

HEBREWS

Written before AD 70, the book of Hebrews reads more like a sermon than a letter. The King James Version of the Bible names Paul as the writer, but manuscripts found later do not name an author.

Hebrews was possibly written to second-generation Christians considering a return to Judaism. These Jewish Christians were likely undergoing physical and social persecution.

Hebrews is pro-Jesus, not anti-Semitic. The writer explains that Jesus is our clearest picture of the nature of God. We learn that (1) God loves us; (2) God wants to forgive us and gives us a second chance when we sin; (3) God has a special affection for the poor, the downtrodden, and children; (4) God has lots of grace but also limits; and (5) God doesn't force himself on us.

Chapter 11 lists the "Heroes of Faith."

JAMES

James, the earliest New Testament book, possibly written in AD 47/48 by James, the brother of Jesus (though scholars debate his identity), is a how-to book on Christian living. This is wisdom literature of the New Testament, offering basic biblical wisdom and advice.

1 PETER

The fisherman Peter, one of the twelve disciples, wrote this letter in approximately AD 62–64. He encourages suffering Christians everywhere but specifically Jewish Christians driven out of Jerusalem who were under severe persecution by the Roman Emperor Nero. Struggling and suffering are part of the human condition. God works through this, not around it. Much wisdom can come from these difficulties.

In 1 Peter 1:6-7, he emphasizes that struggles can glorify Christ.

2 PETER

Peter wrote this second letter around AD 67 to caution the church against corruption and against false teachers. He urges them to grow in faith and knowledge of Christ.

Chapter 3 covers the purpose of the letter and an explanation of the delay of the Lord's second coming.

1 JOHN

The apostle John, likely the only surviving apostle at the time of writing (AD 85–90), wrote this letter from Ephesus. He wrote to a divided community to reassure Christians in their faith and to counter false teachings.

In 1 John 5:13, he explains his purpose for writing.

2 JOHN

Written around the same time as 1 John and 3 John, this letter from the apostle John is a personal note to friends with more warnings about false teachers.

3 JOHN

This is another personal note from the apostle John, this time commending Gaius for his hospitality and encouraging him in his Christian faith.

JUDE

Jude is traditionally considered a brother of Jesus and James, though the writer's identity is uncertain. He wrote around AD 65 to remind the church to remain constantly vigilant, to stay strong in their beliefs, and, without mincing words, to warn them against those who abandon the truth and believe false teachings (see 1:4).

REVELATION

This book is full of visions, prophecies, and dreams. It is the grand finale of the Bible story, describing the ultimate triumph of Christ, along with the new heaven and the new earth.

Written around AD 95/96 by the apostle John as directed by God, this book gives warning and hope to believers.

His point is that complete understanding is not necessary. Readers see God's wrath in this writing, and Jesus comes in at chapter 19.

Key verses about the themes of Revelation are 1:3; 12:10; 14:13; 19:19-21; and 21:1-4.

---

[1] To learn about Martin Luther and the Reformation, as well as other key men in history, see Eric Metaxas with Anne Morse, *7 More Men and the Secret of Their Greatness* (Zondervan, 2020).

PART 3

563 Notes from My Bible

These are some of the actual handwritten notes that appear throughout my Bible. I made them over many years of Bible study, preparing Sunday school lessons, and listening to sermons. Some of them came to me in prayer or quiet time with God.

1. Handle the Bible with great care. Before reading, always pray for the guidance and teaching of the Holy Spirit. Take Deuteronomy 4:2 seriously and strive not to add or take away from God's word. (Also see Revelation 22:18-10.)

2. All scripture is not created equally.

3. Complete understanding is not necessary.

4. You will never know God except the God you know yourself.

5. The Old Testament is essentially a book about a nation, Israel. The New Testament is essentially a book about a Man, Jesus. The nation had to be formed to bring forth the Man.

6. To better understand God, we need a grasp of God's holiness and also the spirit world.

7. No one and nothing can stop God's plan.

8. Having the attitude of Jesus is more important than winning the argument.

9. Humility is an open invitation for the Spirit's presence in our lives.

10. Humility thinks neither too highly nor too lowly of self. It doesn't focus on self at all.

11. Satan is real. His temptations are real.

12. God tests us. Satan tempts us.

13. Terms and expressions and actual words used in the Bible can be different from our everyday usage. Even certain English words have changed meaning since the Bible was written. The Bible contains different types of speech, just like our languages today: symbolism, metaphors, similes, idioms, sarcasm, humor. It is not completely literal.

14. The Bible contains cultural truths and also spiritual and eternal truths.

15. Blessings can come from unexpected places and people.

16. Prayer changes things.

17. Prayer changes me.

18. What occupies most of your thoughts, time, and efforts?

19. Faith usually starts with a whisper. It requires belief and action.

20. Jesus recognized two classes of people—the saved and the lost. He didn't focus on social or political issues.

21. Jesus knew a large part of the world would reject the gospel.

22. The kingdom of heaven is a spiritual realm, not a geographic location.

23. Don't focus on the faults of others.

24. You may fall, but you'll never fail.

25. Focus on God's possibilities, not on the problem and your limitations.

26. Bring your loaves and fish. God will bless and multiply what little you bring.

27. The deity of Jesus is the foundation on which the church rests.

28. The most important work of a church is to preach Christ crucified.

29. God reveals Himself to me through nine different ways: nature, scripture, personal experience, the experiences of others, music, worship services, prayer, dreams, visions and Jesus (God's greatest self-revelation).

30. We are caretakers of God's word.

31. Our relationship with God should define all of our other relationships.

32. You can love someone and not like them.

33. We are commanded to love.

34. Jesus is the visible and tangible image of God.

35. In reading and understanding the Bible, Jesus is the starting place and the ending place.

36. The time to deal with temptations is early on, not later.

37. Hurry, noise, and crowds are tools of the devil.

38. Sin's consequences are not predictable.

39. Some choices are not reversible. We don't know going in.

40. Jesus's suffering is a part of the Christian religion that is not pretty or appealing.

41. To the ancient thinking mind, God's sacrifice of his son Jesus made perfect sense. God had decreed that due to the seriousness of sin, in addition to humility, repentance, confession, and contrition, a blood sacrifice was required. God accepted the substitutionary slaying of an animal (lamb, goat, etc.) in the place of the sinner. Then God sent one final sacrifice, Jesus, the Lamb of God. Those were God's rules, not ours, and He lived by them.

42. The plan of salvation is that, by raising Jesus from the dead, God overcame death for Jesus and for us. God defeated the evil one for Jesus and for us. And, if we simply believe and receive this precious, eternal gift, we are granted everlasting life with God, washed clean in the blood of the Lamb of God. In this, we see the depth of God's love, His amazing grace, and His awesome power.

43. We face a spiritual battle. As you might gather from reading C.S. Lewis's *Screwtape Letters*, everything has a pull to it. Good or evil.

44. The resurrection of Jesus is a historical fact. The Christian religion is based on history *and* faith. It is a religion for thinking people.

45. To put an end to this "pesky" Christian religion, the enemies of Jesus merely needed to disprove the resurrection. To them and my atheist/agnostic friends, I ask them to do something the people of Jesus's day were unable to do: "Show me the body!"

46. Satan always submits to the authority of Jesus.

47. Our expectations change as our faith increases.

48. Human needs trump religious rules.

49. Jesus used logic and not emotion in His attempts to teach and persuade.

50. Spiritual growth is a slow, gradual process.

51. Christianity is not a religion based on healing miracles, but Jesus paid the price for our spiritual healing if we have faith (1 Peter 2:24).

52. What is impossible for us is an opportunity for God.

53. The Holy Spirit empowers us to live in ways we didn't think possible.

54. Glory and suffering go hand and hand.

55. Anything worth having costs something.

56. Human will is not enough to conquer our problems.

57. Jesus had to live and die by faith, just like we do.

58. Compare your actual age to your spiritual age. Our actual age increases over time as we deteriorate, while our spiritual age grows more vigorous and energetic. See 2 Corinthians 4:16.

59. God's calling of Mary was not based on Mary's knowledge of God but on God's knowledge of Mary. He knew her heart.

60. It is possible to serve evil rulers and also be faithful to God.

61. Be motivated by something other than money.

62. Everything has meaning in God's plan.

63. Christ came to give the world something it could not give: true joy and peace.

64. Jesus rejected power and sensationalism.

65. Healing and miracles were not the focus of Jesus's ministry, but they were part of it.

66. As my Mama used to say, "Life is precious. Make it count."

67. Jesus doesn't remain in places where there is fear of His goodness.

68. God calls anybody and everybody who will obey and follow Him.

69. The pace of life and its demands can rob us of the joys of life.

70. Make prayer your first choice.

71. We struggle with defining infinity, but God holds creation in His hands (Psalm 19:1).

72. Christianity came from Judaism.

73. Having children or a pet gives us great insight into God's love for us.

74. When someone shows you who they are, believe them.

75. Choosing to be under God's authority is freedom, not bondage.

76. Happiness is usually dependent on circumstances. Joy is not.

77. In Jesus's "upside-down" world, the last shall be first; we are to serve, not be served; we should seek first the kingdom of God, and all these things shall be added to us (Matthew 6:33); there is healing in brokenness; the poor shall become rich; if we admit our sin and filth, we will be cleansed; the weak shall become strong; we become slaves to God to be free; the gentle and humble shall become bold and renewed; we wanted a conquering warrior, but God sent the Prince of Peace; and, finally, through death there is life—the end is the beginning.

78. Worry and self-centeredness are sins and cause illnesses.

79. Who lives and who dies is not always a measure of righteousness.

80. Life doesn't march to the beat of a moral formula.

81. Jesus doesn't answer the "why" question.

82. God is searching for us.

83. No matter how we got lost, God's love reaches out to us.

84. From the beginning, God set apart male and female: neither exalted, neither depreciated. Humans caused these divisions later.

85. God is a God of order, not confusion.

86. There is a time to throw a big party and be excessive.

87. Any person can restore their relationship with God.

88. Grace offends fairness.

89. God is not limited by time or space.

90. How much time do we spend thanking God?

91. Seeing isn't believing. Believing is seeing.

92. Apologize first, then work on forgiving.

93. God is all we have, need, or want.

94. God's nature is to be merciful.

95. God is not just if He allows evil to stand forever.

96. We all have an appointment with God. Every day, we are one day closer. Knowing this gives meaning to life.

97. To God, a thousand years is like a moment, and vice versa.

98. Human responsibility is never taken away, even in events that God has predetermined.

99. Some people rebel when they don't get what they want.

100. We should not take daily bread for granted.

101. Do you want to know God? Look at Jesus.

102. Consider your witness both now and after you're gone.

103. Down deep, people are looking for a voice to guide and direct them.

104. Christianity is the only religion where God is reaching out to you.

105. Some will choose not to follow. They love darkness more than light.

106. One conversation can change someone's life forever.

107. People don't like being told what to believe or how to act. However, they will observe others and come to their own conclusions.

108. Jesus associated with sinners, social outcasts, and common people. He healed the sick, gave women a prominent role, loved the poor, did not judge, showed kindness and compassion, and was not selfish and power hungry. What's not to love about Him?

109. Be more intentional in your efforts to show your faith for God's glory.

110. Our "loaves" seem inadequate to us, but God blesses them and multiplies them.

111. Leave the results to God. What God wants is obedience.

112. Lord, prepare me for what is being bestowed upon me.

113. Paul wanted to be a missionary in Spain. God gave him what he really needed while he was in prison: the courage to face death. In the end, he wasn't getting out of prison.

114. Jesus fought Satan with scripture.

115. In every situation, Jesus saw an opportunity to glorify God. Humans look for somebody to blame.

116. You are either a fire watcher, a fire starter, or a fire fighter.

117. If everybody likes you, you are doing something wrong.

118. Peace is not the absence of persecution.

119. Expect persecution.

120. Excessive focus on oneself causes a lot of problems.

121. Jesus was bold, resolute, and incredibly intelligent.

122. Peter thought he was willing to die for Jesus. He needed instead to be willing for Jesus to die for him.

123. The most important chapter in the Bible is possibly John 20.

124. The disciples finally learned how to receive forgiveness.

125. There are some things for us not to know.

126. Opposition brings opportunities.

127. Our experiences don't form the basis of the Christian faith. Jesus does.

128. Jesus promised the Spirit would come.

129. Be strong in what you believe. We are messengers, not judges.

130. We want results. God wants a witness.

131. God doesn't usually change us until we are sorry for our past.

132. "Be tough minded and tender hearted" (Dr. Howard Edington).[1]

133. God calls us to grow. Are you the same this year as last year?

134. We were created to ask and receive, just like children.

135. To understand God's character and true nature, we must know how much God hates sin.

136. God has never let me down. My understanding of God has let me down many times.

137. God's will shall be done.

138. Paul met Jesus personally, and his life was never the same.

139. Only in retrospect do we see God's hand, guidance, and timing.

140. How the Christian message is delivered makes a big difference.

141. The true sign of a great leader is doing what God tells you to do even under pressure.

142. Don't flaunt your belief.

143. Accept uncertainty.

144. *Know* God instead of just *knowing of* God.

145. All peoples don't know God because of the way some evangelists and preachers preach; the way we live; the judgment of God; and the callousness of people's hearts.

146. Homophobia is a term used to intimidate. Don't fear or hate those who are different than you.

147. Some love is conditional. God's is not.

148. Sin is so powerful that it can destroy us. God is much more powerful. He can remake us.

149. Our salvation is secure even though we sin. Don't have doubts about your salvation.

150. God doesn't want us to live a defeated life.

151. There is no such thing as my truth; there is one truth.

152. Don't ask or say who will go to heaven or hell.

153. Leave judgment to God.

154. Don't feel weak or like a failure for seeking help.

155. The will of God is made known not when our lives conform to the world but when our minds are transformed.

156. Disagree without being disagreeable.

157. Be your own person as God made you to be.

158. Don't worship people.

159. To some, there is no evil; it's all relative. God decides.

160. We can have tolerance without acceptance or endorsement.

161. The heart knows things the head doesn't.

162. We are to confront open sin.

163. The Romans were tolerant of everything…except Christianity.

164. If you and I talk long enough, we will discover things we disagree about and also things we agree on.

165. Jesus had more trouble with established religious institutions than with typical sinners.

166. Correct your misunderstandings.

167. Nothing is worthwhile without love.

168. What holds a church together is not the building or our gifts. It's the Savior, Jesus.

169. Our faith is meaningless and powerless without the resurrection.

170. God's motive is always love for God's children.

171. We focus on the experience of death. God wants us to focus on the change from this life to the next.

172. Nothing you do for the Lord is useless.

173. The resurrected body is a spiritual body energized by the spirit of God, fit for life with God.

174. What are your personal values and priorities?

175. Pray for God's grace daily, not just occasionally.

176. Wrong motives and methods can render Christian service invalid.

177. We all have an area of service and influence in God's plan and in God's time.

178. After a long period of tradition, change comes slowly, while criticism comes quickly.

179. Christians owe basic respect to both believers and non-believers.

180. Paul is living proof that God can call whomever God wants.

181. Anything important requires powers of thought and concentration.

182. Having a purpose guards you against boredom, fatigue, and discouragement.

183. Make sure you succeed in the right things.

184. The bigger we make God, the smaller our problems become.

185. When you are losing steam, read Philippians 4.

186. Don't tolerate toxic thoughts.

187. How does what you experience compare with the teaching of Jesus?

188. You are not what you think you are. What you think, you are.

189. If God prompts us, God will enable us.

190. The true nature of the call of Christ is to serve and share.

191. Because Paul went to prison, we have Ephesians, Philippians, Colossians, and Philemon.

192. It's not the words of the gospel but the power behind the gospel that changed the world.

193. The greatest need of the church today might be to recover the wonder, the awe, and the joy of God's word.

194. We must depend totally on God's grace, not our works.

195. God can use your story. Everybody has one.

196. Choose to be thankful.

197. When I pray, many times God tells me simple answers to some of my most perplexing problems. It is mysterious and amazing when this happens.

198. God does not allow us to fulfill all our desires.

199. Disapprove the practice, but don't condemn or judge the person.

200. No matter the question at hand, ask yourself, "Is it essential to salvation?" Jesus is focused on salvation.

201. God not only forgives but also forgets!

202. Christianity abolished slavery.

203. Truth is timeless. Culture is not.

204. Focus on God's strength to endure, not yours.

205. A quest for excellence is a quest for power. Use it wisely.

206. The Bible is our standard for testing everything else. It protects us from false teachings and shows us how to live.

207. Unless we know the scriptures, our discussions and beliefs drift into opinion. Always come back to the Bible, and filter it through Jesus.

208. Sometimes good causes must wait while greater causes take precedence.

209. We can only control ourselves. We can't make someone do what they do not want to do. That is God's job.

210. God is already working in the lives of people we are trying to reach.

211. Only through God's influence and love can we accept/forgive others, especially those who have wronged us.

212. As much as possible, be tolerant and respectful of other cultures and religions, but don't back down from what you know and believe. Jesus is the only way to eternal life. Don't bargain this away. Christ is superior to everyone and everything. Christianity supersedes all other religions and can never be surpassed. We cannot find anything better. I know this sounds high-handed and arrogant. I do not mean it that way. It is simply the truth. Christianity is not anti-anything. It is simply pro-Jesus.

213. The closer you look at Jesus, the better you like Him.

214. Jesus refused to be intimidated.

215. We become frustrated trying to have more faith, but it is a gift that is a byproduct of knowing God.

216. Faith is the assurance of things hoped for and the conviction of things not seen (Hebrews 11:1).

217. To finally take God at His word is a real relief and act of faith.

218. The beginning point of faith is believing that God is who He says He is. The ending point of faith is believing in God's promises.

219. Faith is not the absence of doubt but the steps taken in spite of it.

220. Wisdom is knowledge guided by understanding.

221. Wisdom comes from obedience, not pursuing knowledge.

222. Faith allows us to entrust our most priceless possessions to God (even our children).

223. A peacemaker is not always peaceable.

224. To have peace, we need to deal with every sin in our lives.

225. What really makes us happy and gives us true joy? Knowing we are doing God's will.

226. We do not have the right to demand that people approve of what we believe or how we act.

227. The Bible starts with "In the beginning…" and ends with "Amen." In between those two are the most important things you need to know.

228. Temptation comes from evil desires inside us.

229. To tempt is to try to make somebody do something, to entice sin. A test is an examination or trial. God does not tempt us. He does test us.

230. Turn trials into opportunities.

231. Arrogant or angry people are not wise.

232. God and Satan are contending for our souls.

233. Live this year as if it's the last one you will live.

234. Secular "holiness" or morality is based on social, cultural, and personal standards. Its source is what humans can do on their own. Christian holiness grows out of the unchanging holiness of God. Its source and strength are God.

235. Pascal, French philosopher and mathematician (1623–1662), developed the modern theory of probability: "I prefer to believe those writers who

get their throats cut for what they write." I include this quote because I have the same thoughts about Christian martyrs.

236. Beware of spiritual dangers around you.

237. The disciples spoke and wrote what they saw and heard.

238. Look to Jesus for your understanding of scripture.

239. There has been a delay of the second coming of Jesus, but we are 2,000 years closer than the people who knew Him as a Man on earth.

240. The first judgment of the world was water. The second judgment will be fire. See 2 Peter 3:6-7.

241. The people in Noah's day mocked him and didn't believe in the flood.

242. In the second judgment, God's people will be delivered. For non-believers, it will be sudden and terrible.

243. Jesus hinted that His return could take a long time (Matthew 25:19). Also, see 2 Peter 3:8-9

244. It's easy to be misled by clever and attractive arguments.

245. God is sovereign over time and history.

246. Love and goodness win in the end.

247. Life makes sense.

248. Be patient.

249. God is not in a hurry.

250. Wait faithfully and expectantly.

251. Decisions are important, and they matter.

252. Trust that God has it together and under control.

253. Christian love is not a feeling. It is a command and a choice.

254. In the symbolism of the Old Testament, you transfer your sins to an animal that is sacrificed. In the New Testament, the sacrifice is Jesus.

255. A transformed life does not mean perfection.

256. God doesn't ask us to agree with him but to obey him.

257. Christianity is a religion of the heart and the mind.

258. You can love your brother and sister before getting your theology straight.

259. There is nothing our children can do to make us love them any less.

260. Tough love tells the truth, forgives but demands a change, sets boundaries, won't take personal abuse, backs off when appropriate, and stays strong.

261. Soft love tells what someone wants to hear, removes responsibility, and gives excuses.

262. There is no middle ground. We either belong to God and obey him or we live under Satan's control.

263. We want clear standards for deciding between right and wrong so we can make the best choices. The Bible is our source for this and helps us identify false teachers.

264. Some people use the right words but change their meanings.

265. Truth eventually comes out.

266. Be true to yourself as God intended. If you are at peace with yourself, you are a comfort and blessing to those around you. This is a terrific witness. Don't underestimate it.

267. Observe the fruits that are produced in a person's life.

268. Merely knowing the error of your ways doesn't mean you will reform.

269. We ignore God's warnings and previous judgments.

270. Reaching those who don't know Christ can often be difficult but at times is surprisingly easy.

271. Show compassion.

272. What God promises will come about.

273. God has never totally abandoned His people and never will.

274. Simple history: the Roman empire passed away, while the church survived (like Jesus said).

275. Does history have any meaning and purpose without God?

276. The Christian view of life and history is different from the world's. Jesus is coming again, and then there will be judgment. This makes sense of life. Ultimately, good and evil are dealt with.

277. When Jesus decides to fight, it's over quickly.

278. God's judgment is not cruel or vindictive. It's morally right and makes good sense.

279. Be humble enough to accept God's authority over your life.

280. We are God's creation. God has a claim on us. Everything is His. He could have created anything, but He chose us and this world.

281. What God made is not an accident. God had a plan.

282. God chose relationship over isolation.

283. Sin affects people and creation.

284. Women need men to be respectful, caring, supportive, loving, and loyal. Men need women to be respectful, caring, supportive, loving, and loyal.

285. God saw the wickedness of the world not as an angry tyrant but as a troubled Parent.

286. God intended the world to be a place of order, peace, fun, happiness, love, and worship.

287. God always has a people.

288. Abraham believed with his heart and his feet.

289. Abraham's story is not really about Abraham. It's about God.

290. We prefer to walk by sight, not by faith, but that is not God's way.

291. Be careful what you believe. Powerful things can happen.

292. God wants us to trust him. He can do the rest.

293. We forfeit a lot of peace through worry, doubt, and fear.

294. God uses good and bad circumstances and allows certain events to happen, but we are still responsible for our actions. There is always a way out of temptation.

295. What are you willing to lose to get what you want? If we leave God out of it, we still feel empty.

296. Some of what God has to work with isn't pretty.

297. We all have the ability to bless.

298. Sometimes we should stop talking about God and begin talking to Him and listening to Him.

299. The toughest battle is sometimes against ourselves. Excessive focus on oneself, on the outcome, or on our opponent results in failure.

300. Strong faith overcomes panic.

301. Find the right way to live peacefully without accepting or accommodating a "foreign god" culture.

302. Joseph's obedience in the "small areas" prepared him for the bigger issues.

303. To flee temptations, practice faithfulness.

304. The mature, thinking believer recognizes God at work when others don't.

305. We might not know the plan, but we can know God's laws.

306. Turning to government rather than God leads to slavery, not freedom. Government can become our master.

307. The government is not our deliverer; God is.

308. Success is hard on many people. They don't handle it well. The same is true for companies, churches, and nations.

309. The best eyesight is 50/20 (Genesis 50:20).

310. God brought the slave nation out of Egypt for a reason: to redeem the world.

311. In the Old Testament, we see God through the eyes of Moses.

312. God used the Israelites to bring us salvation and redeem the world.

313. The central event in the Old Testament is the exodus.

314. God chose Moses even though he was far from perfect.

315. Today, in thousands of synagogues on Friday nights, Moses shapes the Jewish mind. A Jew looks at God through the revelations of Moses. Muslims get their revelations from Muhammad. A Christian looks at God through the revelations of Jesus.

316. Throughout the Bible, we see the influence of mothers.

317. God did not change Moses's personality and who he was. God molded his abilities and strengths to do God's will.

318. Moses officially got God's call at age eighty.

319. Accepting God's call brings blessings and difficulties. Expect them both.

320. There is a time to get up from your prayers and do something.

321. God doesn't give up on us when our faith falters.

322. When we can do the job ourselves, we tend to forget about God.

323. We take so many things for granted. When is the last time you thanked God for oxygen?

324. In circumstances that generate fear, we have the greatest opportunity to witness the power of God.

325. People are not talked into faith and belief. Events, circumstances, and actions draw people to it.

326. Always give thanks for your food.

327. Watch out for big government (Genesis 47:13-26).

328. The Ten Commandments free us to live with joy and hope. Jesus fulfilled the commandments:

329. The basis for the Commandments is reverence for God.

330. Jesus interprets the Commandments in Matthew 5:21-48.

331. The Commandments are for our sake, not God's.

332. Good leaders give orders rather than take them.

333. Children suffer for the sins of their parents: alcoholism, child abuse, selfishness, greed, and more.

334. We treat sin casually. The consequences are not limited.

335. The Pharisees were overzealous in applying the code from Leviticus.

336. The law teaches, but it doesn't save.

337. Without Leviticus, the powerful message of the cross is not fully understood.

338. Think before you speak.

339. The power of unity is amazing.

340. Your personal wilderness includes transitioning between jobs, marriages, homes, levels of health, and stages of life.

341. The easy thing to do: complain, criticize, be cynical, look for shortcuts.

342. The safe thing to do: go with God, claim God's promises, trust, be faithful.

343. We don't have to do it all on our own. God sends help.

344. Never get a fishing trip confused with catching fish.

345. The Israelites thought occupying the promised land was all about them. They missed the point. It was really all about God.

346. Israel disappointed God one too many times.

347. Everybody gets mad. Worse yet, God gets mad.

348. There are two conditions to God's mercy on earth: (1) obedience and (2) continued ethical conduct.

349. Tragedy can lead to transformation and positive change.

350. The Hebrews' story is our story.

351. Tell your story.

352. Prosperity, more than poverty, dulls our spiritual vision and senses.

353. We look for God's hand instead of God's face.

354. Change produces stress, anxiety, and emotion and makes smart people do dumb things.

355. It's not how you start but how you finish that matters.

356. The best rewards of life go to those who work, sacrifice, and obey God.

357. God was supposed to be the direct ruler of Israel (a theocracy). They didn't take God seriously.

358. Every man did what was right in his eyes. Sound familiar?

359. God used evil people to punish Israel for their sins.

360. God's commandments don't change.

361. Israel didn't keep their religious and cultural life strong. But there was a remnant.

362. God's plans are never defeated. Don't get in God's way. But there was a remnant.

363. Be available to God and to others.

364. There is a point for everyone where we cry out to God.

365. Go in the strength you have, dependent on God.

366. After you make the decision, act on it.

367. God doesn't think like we do. Try to discover God's mind.

368. It's okay to seek God's reassurance but beware of Satan's influence.

369. We are at our best when we are true to God, not when we look for success on our own.

370. The Israelites neglected worship of God and wanted a peaceful coexistence with the Canaanites at any cost. They became envious of the prosperity of the Canaanites and credited Baal for the fertility of the land, made political alliances with an attitude of "let's be like them," and disobeyed God by intermarrying with people who served idols.

371. God wants us to follow and obey without knowing the consequences.

372. God was at work for them, but Israel did not see it or know it much of the time.

373. Don't be a control freak. Trust God.

374. There is a time to grieve. Then there is a time to make a painful choice to leave the past and its hurt behind and move into the present and future that God has planned for you.

375. Whatever you do, do it well. People will notice.

376. Don't miss the message by getting hung up on the small stuff.

377. Bach said, "At a reverent performance of music, God is always at hand with his gracious presence."[2]

378. With Saul, David proved that there is a time to walk away from relationships.

379. If you expect God's blessings, you must follow God's word.

380. To cut out distractions, God will take us aside.

381. God blesses those obedient to him. There is judgment on those disobedient to him.

382. But bad things happen to all. What's the difference?

383. The writers who wrote about Israel were sure of one thing: the nation split and the kingdoms fell as punishment for their sins—idolatry and careless attitudes towards God's laws. God's people did not separate and distinguish themselves from the religious practices of the others around them.

384. Your major assignment in life is to become the person God created you to be. No one else has your assignment.

385. First, give thanks.

386. Worship is essential for a vital relationship with God.

387. Handling wealth, power, and praise can be challenging. Beware.

388. Don't take criticism personally.

389. We focus on the drought. God focuses on the opportunity.

390. Obedience to God results in the confrontation of evil.

391. Much of the Bible contrasts those who live for God and those who don't.

392. In Christ, we lose some battles, but we do win the war.

393. God has a use for us regardless of our past.

394. From God's viewpoint, our problems don't seem quite as bad.

395. Elijah had a hard life with tough work to do. His mission was to drive Baalism out of Israel. He thought his life was a failure. God didn't see it that way.

396. Faith does not panic.

397. "God is not worried." (Dr. John Haggai)

398. A nation's leadership impacts the spiritual commitment of its people.

399. Overall, the Hebrew people had been moving further and further away from their history, heritage, and core beliefs. This bad trend is hard to stop and is happening in many nations today.

400. Never underestimate the importance of teaching children.

401. Renew and refresh covenants to keep them healthy (marriage, children, friendships).

402. Israel and Judah became a "me" generation. There was no sanctity of life, they worshiped other gods, they didn't honor or remember the Sabbath, their judicial system became lax, and taxes were raised time and time again. They prospered materially but not spiritually.

403. God finally judged Israel and Judah, and they couldn't believe it was happening. The same will happen to modern nations that neglect their spiritual health.

404. Sometimes we focus too much on God's mercy and grace and not enough on God's justice and judgment.

405. Some of the original terrorists were the Assyrians and Babylonians.

406. King David's first act was establishing Jerusalem as the capital city.

407. God will allow you to go your own way.

408. Jesus's first response is to forgive those who are against him. No other religion does this.

409. Arrive at church prepared and ready to hear a word from God.

410. If you were driven away from your home by a foreign adversary, what would you miss most?

411. Lead yourself first and have a mission that matters. Be a big thinker, ethical, open to change, a team player, a team builder, committed, and loyal. Create change, take risks, make decisions, be courageous, communicate, and use power wisely.

412. Don't use language that offends God or other people.

413. God's work sometimes looks like coincidences.

414. Nothing good is likely to be done in a hurry.

415. Fear reveals where our hearts are and what we are most devoted to.

416. Gather the facts, focus on the real issue, examine the alternatives and motives, decide on a course of action, and act.

417. God works through ordinary people. His silence is not detachment.

418. What you reap, you will sow.

419. God is present. Let's celebrate!

420. Don't blame God.

421. C. S. Lewis wrote, "If you want a religion to make you comfortable, I certainly don't recommend Christianity."[3]

422. Life is a complex mixture of fear and sadness, joy and celebration. Don't let the hard times rob you of opportunities to celebrate the good times.

423. I don't have all the answers.

424. I don't need all the answers. God has them.

425. Don't judge others who are suffering. In fact, don't judge others.

426. Freedom is beautiful and also dangerous. God allows things to happen, but he doesn't cause bad things to happen.

427. Prayer takes many forms. Don't make it superstitious; make it real. God is not a deal maker or an order taker.

428. Abraham Lincoln said, "I can see how it might be possible for a man to look down upon the earth and be an atheist, but I cannot conceive how he could look up into the heavens and say there is no God."

429. What do we want for our children and grandchildren? We want to see them playing, having fun, laughing, loving, and communicating with us. God wants the same from his children.

430. Some of our religious thoughts should change or be tweaked over the years.

431. Are you stuck in the anger stage? Why?

432. The person who never knew the presence of God won't feel or miss God's absence.

433. God's peace is our weapon against Satan.

434. Church, unfortunately, is made up of people, some whom we don't like and all of them sinners—including us. It's kind of like every place we've ever worked.

435. When our desire for God dominates our hearts, our minds will focus on serving and worshiping him. The heart has the greater wisdom. The story of the prodigal son taught me this (Luke 15:11-32).

436. We place limits on our forgiveness. God does not.

437. Like burnt offerings, our religious activities are sometimes used to cover up our sins.

438. Cast your burdens upon the Lord, and leave them there.

439. God is a God of second chances.

440. God's abundance comes when we gain wisdom and knowledge of God.

441. The Psalmist, too, struggled with the question of "why."

442. Be careful of the prosperity gospel.

443. Go beyond your childhood idea of worship.

444. Satan's probable thought process: "In the next generation there is always hope."

445. There is a spiritual dimension to a country's well-being.

446. In addition to reading God's word, meditate on it.

447. Problems often get the best of us. Youth get discouraged when they see this happen to adults.

448. One of the purposes of church is to work together for God.

449. Don't ever compare yourself to others.

450. Wealth provides opportunities to care for others.

451. Jesus' messages on wealth:
 a. Matthew 6:19-24
 b. Matthew 13:22
 c. Mark 10:23
 d. Luke 16:13

452. Live for a cause greater than yourself.

453. Not all of Solomon's ideas were God's ideas.

454. It's not what you know; it's who you know.

455. Make decisions and put some order in your life.

456. God promises salvation, wholeness, and peace, not physical healing and prosperity. He watched his Son die.

457. God has some things to say to the nations who have abused his chosen people. Those who mistreat Israel will not go unpunished. History bears this out.

458. The one who shouts is usually losing the argument.

459. Never argue with an idiot. A passerby will not be able to tell the difference between you and the idiot.

460. In a battle between spiritual vs. physical, spiritual wins every time.

461. We should consult God about every decision we make.

462. God is not out to get us. God is out to find us.

463. God sees us differently than we see ourselves.

464. Make the present moment count.

465. God will restore Israel and Jerusalem. It's part of God's plan.

466. The big picture is that God had a plan of salvation for humanity's ultimate redemption (See the thumbnail sketch of Israel's history at my summary of the book of Ezekiel.)

467. Indifference to the poor is a big deal in God's eyes.

468. Whatever your situation, don't abandon your core convictions.

469. We trust ourselves too much and God too little.

470. Watch out when people say overly nice things about you (friend or enemy).

471. God is watching. God knows your heart.

472. When do we become responsible for our actions? When we are capable of realizing their effects.

473. The nation of Israel was deceived.

474. Develop a deeper awareness of God's presence.

475. We can lose the ability to recognize sin.

476. God gives each of us individually enough revelation to establish responsibility.

477. God blesses us to be a blessing to others and to give God glory.

478. If you were God, how would you like to be worshiped?

479. Remember: We are God's children.

480. The five stages of grief are denial, anger, bargaining, depression, and acceptance.[4]

481. God wanted to tear down the wall between Jews and Gentiles. People want to build walls between each other.

482. A thought becomes an attitude becomes an action.

483. The most effective way to share the gospel is to have a right relationship with God, yourself, and others.

484. Talk with God about anything.

485. There is a difference between quick and soon.

486. One of the great paradoxes in scripture is to depend on the Lord yet at the same time use the talents and abilities God gives us to accomplish the work God gives us to do.

487. A level of excellence and performance in any field can actually become an obstacle in seeing God's power.

488. Your soul is the immaterial part of you. It is reflected in your personality. It can be self-centered. The Spirit is an immaterial being. It exists exclusively for God. (We are told to worship God in spirit and in truth; John 4:24. Ezekiel 36:26-27 also helps me understand this).

489. Both the soul and spirit leave the body at death.

490. It takes work to live by God's standards.

491. Going through the motions in worship or in anything is dangerous.

492. Every Sunday in churches around the world, two kinds of Christians gather in church. The unblessed want to win God's favor. The blessed gather because they already have it. One comes out of obligation and fear; the other comes in gratitude and celebration.

493. There is a fine line between not worrying or being anxious and not doing anything about your circumstances. Take some action.

494. When God is slow to answer, what we really believe about Him is revealed.

495. For some, Jesus is their Savior but not Lord of their life.

496. Always look for the problem behind the problem—the real problem.

497. The cross reveals the heart of God. This is God's nature.

498. You are the expert on one thing: your relationship with God and Christ's influence on you. Your story is real.

499. We can't do God's work well if we can't express His kind of forgiveness.

500. If a person denies biblical truths, God's existence, or our spiritual nature, they are either ignorant or arrogant or both.

501. Losing your Lord and finding Him again is a powerful experience, as Peter knew.

502. God made us simple, but we have made ourselves very complicated.

503. We are made to communicate with God.

504. Be a God-pleaser, not a people-pleaser.

505. There is power in reading the Bible.

506. Analyze scripture: What does it say? What does it mean? What does it teach us about God? What does Jesus say about it? How can I apply it today to my life?

507. Gifts of the Holy Spirit include wisdom, understanding, counsel, strength, knowledge of the Lord, fear of the Lord, delight in the fear of the Lord (Isaiah 11:2-3), love, joy, peace, patience, kindness, goodness, faithfulness, gentleness, self-control (Galatians 5:22-23), power, and the ability to witness (Acts 1:8).

508. Jesus's actions and words shape the image we have of Him, not His physical appearance.

509. Give me the gift of quiet reflection.

510. Make biblical decisions, not cultural ones.

511. Five standards of being a Christian include:
    a. Obey God's Commandments.
    b. Recognize the presence of the Holy Spirit in your life.
    c. Nurture a growing understanding and as you seek a deeper relationship with Christ.
    d. Live a life consistent with Christ's life.
    e. Cultivate an inner peace.

512. God doesn't give many directions. He does give lots of advice in his "Instruction Book," but when it comes to his will, we have freedom.

513. What is the role of the church to enable us to encounter God?
   a. Provide a worship experience and activities that connect people to God.
   b. Teach the Bible.
   c. Offer pastoral care that heals and creates fellowship.
   d. Do missions (hands-on and financial).

514. Understand that a steady Sunday job or activity can break a good habit of church attendance. The Bible teaches us to attend church and take a day of rest. It's unwise not to obey this. We need fellowship and support from other believers.

515. Think of God as Creator, Comforter, Savior, Friend, Deliverer, Healer, Hiding Place, Hope, Leader, Sure Foundation, Defender, Guide, Peace, and Counselor.

516. Live in the knowledge that God is watching and cares for us.

517. We must experience the presence of God in both the darkest moments of life and the times of celebration.

518. These were the principles of Paul's ministry (and are still common courtesy): find common ground; avoid a know-it-all attitude; make others feel accepted; be sensitive to the needs and concerns of others; look for ways and opportunities to tell others about Christ.

519. God is Lord over us. We are God's servants. This goes against everything our culture teaches us.

520. There is power and purpose behind nature. The universe did not just happen. The charge of an electron, the strength of gravity, the mass of a proton—if these or other constants were the tiniest bit different, atoms would not hold together, stars would not burn, and there would be no life.

521. The Bible acknowledges the passing pleasures of sin (Hebrews 11:24-25).

522. These are the qualities of a good leader:
   a. Not swayed by popular opinion
   b. Predicts deliverance

    c. Lays out a course of action
    d. Initiates action
    e. Motivates
    f. Points to God
    g. Keeps the mission and goals in the forefront

523. Coach Chuck Daly said, "Once you get a taste of where you really want to go, motivation takes care of itself."

524. Give because of a relationship with God and not an end unto itself.

525. Jesus convicts us, but he doesn't condemn us.

526. Satan got Adam and Eve out of God's authority.

527. Satan submits to the authority of Jesus.

528. Don't dwell on the past.

529. All religions but Christianity emphasize works.

530. Jesus supported and promoted the idea of freedom in religion (Luke 9:46-50).

531. Faith comes from being in the presence of Jesus.

532. We are motivated by fear or by love.

533. When God reveals something to us, it's an invitation to join Him.

534. Make slow, quiet decisions.

535. Proceed with humility in matters of faith.

536. God works with whomever He chooses.

537. Difficult times make us value life and appreciate the simple things we take for granted.

538. Even death works in us to bring new perspectives and new life. We move forward in ways we never would without the experience. It reveals our great dependence on God and, ideally, leads to greater faith.

539. God needs time to prepare us for an assignment.

540. Are you and your actions formed by influence or purpose?

541. Situations of suffering can produce good fruit: confirmation of love, humility, courage, patience, greatness of heart, fellowship, and expressions of caring.

542. Jesus loves us without any motive.

543. God is all we have.

544. God is all we need.

545. God is all we want.

546. Satan majors in four things: noise, hurry, crowds, darkness.

547. Accept the gift of forgiveness and salvation.

548. All relationships are based on trust. God trusts us, regardless of if or how we trust him.

549. Cultivating a spirit of gratitude to God
    a. Makes us aware of God's presence.
    b. Makes us look for God's purpose.
    c. Brings our will in submission to God's will.
    d. Reminds us of our dependence on God.
    e. Helps us develop a stronger trust in God.
    f. Teaches that it is essential for us to rejoice (regardless of our situation).
    g. Impacts our witness.
    h. Focuses our attention on God and not our circumstances.
    i. Energizes us.
    j. Transforms our anxiety into peace.
    k. Is great therapy.

550. A positive, optimistic, enthusiastic attitude fills our hearts with thankfulness and increases our opportunities and chances for success and happiness.

551. Create your own environment.

552. In prayer, focus first on God, then our concerns for and relationship with others, and then our relationship to God.

553. Prayer and worship are privileges.

554. Quit working for God's love and start celebrating it.

555. Temptation is not a sin and doesn't disappoint God.

556. Why does God save us by faith alone without works?

557. Faith eliminates pride. Faith isn't a deed we do.

558. Faith exalts God, not me.

559. Faith is an admission that I need help. I can't do it on my own.

560. Faith is based on our relationship with God, not on our performance for God. (Think of boarding a plane and your faith in the pilot and crew.)

561. How to best interpret the Bible divides a lot of us.

562. "What we focus on has us."[5]

563. It's a great moment when we realize who we are.

---

[1] Heard in a sermon by Dr. Edington at Providence Presbyterian Church, Hilton Head Island, SC.

[2] "One Musician Says Bach's Music Has a special Place in Easter," *NPR: All Things Considered*, March 27, 2016, https://www.npr.org/2016/03/27/472067235/one-musician-says-bachs-music-has-a-special-place-in-easter.

[3] C. S. Lewis, *Mere Christianity* (Geoffrey Bles, 1952).

[4] Behnay Books, *The Five Stages of Grief: A Comprehensive and Insightful Guide to the Grief and Loss Process*, audiobook, 2022.

[5] Eugenia Price, quoted in Nell W. Mohney, "Whatever Gets Your Attention, Gets You," *Chattanooga News Free Press*, no date.

PART 4

Favorite Bible Verses

As I read through the Bible the first time, these verses stuck with me in a special way. I focused on some of the verses for specific reasons, for example, the Ten Commandments. I memorized them and thought about them every day. The Joshua passage spoke to me because of situations I went through at work. As for Psalm 19:1, I spend a lot of time outdoors in nature—fishing, walking, birdwatching—and I read this verse to our daughters, Anna and Jordan, at bedtime when we went camping. Proverbs 3:5-6 opened me up to communicate more clearly with God. John 14:23 made me realize I didn't really know God's word. Other verses offered special inspiration and comfort: Matthew 11:28-30; John 14:27; Psalm 34:7; Philippians 4:4-9; 1 Thessalonians 5:16-18. All the verses spoke to me in a meaningful way at a particular time, and they still do.

Exodus 20:1-17—The Ten Commandments

Deuteronomy 14:26—We are meant to have fun!

Joshua 1:7-9—An encouragement to be strong and courageous

1 Samuel 15:22—What the Lord really wants from us

1 Samuel 16:7—"Don't judge a book by its cover."

2 Chronicles 7:14—The "four/three" formula

2 Chronicles 15:2—A promise and a warning

2 Chronicles 16:9—The Lord sees us always and knows us.

Psalm 19:1—The camping verse

Psalm 23—Our weapon against Satan and death, providing peace

Psalm 34:7—Assurance when in trouble

Psalm 34:19—When nothing goes right

Psalm 37:1-8—My Fort Jackson verses

Psalm 55:22—My "fishing verse"

Psalm 91:1—A privilege and a responsibility

Psalm 91:11-12—On angels

Psalm 101:3—Try with all your might not to hate anyone.

Psalm 104:33-34—My "before church service" verses

Psalm 119:27—Meditation

Psalm 119:89—The Lord's word is settled.

Psalm 126:5-6—Keep going even when you don't feel like it. Press on.

Psalm 147:11—Wait for it.

Proverbs 3:5-6—God answered me directly after I kept repeating these verses.

Proverbs 14:26—To get confidence

Proverbs 16:3—The secret to my company's success

Proverbs 23:1-7—Your goals should be motivated by something other than money.

Isaiah 11:2-3—Some gifts of the Spirit

Isaiah 26:3—You will be kept in peace if your thoughts are on God.

Isaiah 40:28-31—Keep on keepin' on.

Isaiah 48:17-18—Pay attention. Obey.

Isaiah 66:1-2—To get God's attention

Daniel 3:17-18 – I love this faith in God no matter what happens.

Jeremiah 29:11-13—God's plan for you

Jeremiah 33:3—Try this. It really works!

Micah 6:8—The Micah manifesto, short and simple

Zechariah 4:6—A great, truthful paradox

Matthew 11:28-30—For the rest you need

John 14:13-17—Prayer is not about me.

John 14:23—The verse that changed my life

John 14:26—Always ask for this help when reading the Bible.

John 14:27—The real peace

John 15:7—Carefully obey this in prayer.

Acts 7:23—Be careful about what enters your mind.

Acts 22:14-15—The key to being a witness

Romans 12:1-2—Don't try to be like everybody else.

Romans 13:1—Show respect.

Ephesians 3:11-21—Scripture building to a stirring crescendo

Ephesians 6:10-17—To fight Satan

Philippians 4:4-9—Don't worry, be happy!

Philippians 4:13—Believe this.

Philippians 4:19—God knows our needs.

Colossians 3:1-17—To develop focus

1 Thessalonians 5:16-18—These short verses got me through a lot.

Hebrews 11:1—Faith defined

Hebrews 11:6—You've gotta have faith.

James 1:5-6—Ask with confidence.

James 1:12—Be tough.

James 4:1-3—Why prayers don't get answered

James 4:4-17—How to draw nearer to God

1 Peter 5:6-7—Humility rewarded

Revelation 1:3—How to be blessed

Luke 1:37—Never give up

Matthew 7:1—Don't judge others. That's God's business.

John 8:32 – Freedom from guilt, fear, and emptiness.

EPILOGUE

It has been a privilege and an honor to have this opportunity to share parts of my life with you. I originally intended this book only for our daughters, Anna and Jordan. I wanted them to be able to look at the many notes in my Bible and not only read and understand them but also to know me and the Lord further in a deeper and meaningful way. As I began the task, it occurred to me that God, through the Holy Spirit, was directing me to a larger audience who could learn eternal and practical truths that the Bible sets before us. Hopefully, this book has not only taken some of the mystery out of the mystery but has given you hope, direction, energy, wisdom, and peace that we as God's children are meant to have. May it help you reach your full potential in life. Along the way, have fun, be joyful, and don't ever pass up the opportunity to have a snow cone!

ABOUT THE AUTHOR

Al Brown is a resident of St. Simons Island, Georgia. After graduating from the University of Georgia in 1972, he began a five-decade career in real estate. He now owns his own real estate company. He is still working to support his bass fishing habit.

Asked to describe himself in a few brief words, Al replied, "In 1982, I was a founding member of the Golden Isles Chamber Music Festival. That same year I placed second in the Brunswick Exchange Club tobacco-spitting contest."

Al grew up in Elberton, a small town in northeast Georgia, the son of hardworking parents. His mother was a homemaker and his father the city manager. He attended the local Baptist church, was an average student who loved music, and enjoyed the outdoors, hunting, hiking, fishing, camping, baseball, basketball, and spending time with family.

Raised in the country with the ability to roam several hundred acres in rural Elbert County, Georgia, even as a boy, Al would get out of bed before his parents, two sisters, and brother and head for the woods to explore and seek out wildlife. Something in the woods called him. He inherited from his mother a happy, easygoing demeanor with a desire to get along and accept people as they are; from his father a quick sense of humor, the ability to tell a joke, and a discerning mind to analyze and simplify people and situations. From them both, he got a can-do attitude with the spirit to survive no matter the odds. They instilled in him respect for elders, a sense of honor to be a member of the Brown family, and the responsibilities and expectations of proper behavior it brought. To this day, he doesn't want to disappoint them, even though they've been gone for some time.

Al's personal values are servanthood, truth, purpose, loyalty, and performance. These carry forward to his business as well.

Al says he's a drinking Baptist. He has taught Sunday school for forty-nine years at First Baptist Church of St. Simons Island, where he plays drums for the choir.

He and his wife Gayle have been married for fifty-two years. They have two daughters, Anna and Jordan, two sons-in-law, both named George, and a grandson, Parker Felton Moore, who is seven years old. Parker caught his first fish at nine months of age, with a little help from Papa.

CREDITS/ACKNOWLEDGMENTS

Mama

Daddy

Gayle Brown

Tom Brown

Marie Cleveland

Dr. Felix Haynes

Ralph and Bonnie Jean Small

Ann and Earl Swicord

Nick Doster

Dr. Ben Haygood

Dr. Bill Henderson

Dr. John Harris Harper

Present and prior members of the
Love Joy Laughter Sunday School Class,
St. Simons Island, GA

SPECIAL ACKNOWLEDGMENTS

I am indebted to Henry H. Halley, Halley's Bible Handbook (Zondervan, 2014) for biblical interpretation and background. I also relied on the Formations Teaching Guide and the Formations Commentary by Smyth & Helwys Publishing, Macon, GA.

Heartfelt thanks to Judy Scarlett, my Executive Assistant. Judy was my first hire when I started my company in 2013. She has evolved from employee to family member as far as the Browns are concerned. We love her. Thank you, Judy, for the many hours you spent on this book and for your loyalty, encouragement, and insights.

Special thanks to Good Faith Media for publishing *Notes from My Father's Bible*. You took on a first-time author and guided me through the process with care and professionalism.

To my wife Gayle, thank you for your patience and understanding as I toiled away on this book for many years. God blessed me with you for a life partner. And thank you for saying "Yes" when I asked you to dance in 1967!

www.ingramcontent.com/pod-product-compliance
Lightning Source LLC
Chambersburg PA
CBHW071007160426
43193CB00012B/1956